MAJESTIC METROPOLITAN LIVING

# MAJESTIC METROPOLITAN LIVING

## VISIONARY HOMES IN THE HEART OF CITIES

**SUE HOSTETLER**

PHOTOGRAPHS BY PETER CHRISTIANSEN VALLI

Clarkson Potter/Publishers
New York

Published in the United States by Clarkson Potter/Publishers, an imprint of the Crown Publishing Group,

a division of Random House, Inc., New York.

www.crownpublishing.com

www.clarksonpotter.com

CLARKSON POTTER is a trademark and POTTER with colophon is a registered trademark of Random House, Inc.

Library of Congress Cataloging-in-Publication Data

Hostetler, Sue.

Majestic metropolitan living / Sue Hostetler. — 1st ed.

1. Interior decoration.    I. Title.

NK2115.H527   2009

747—dc22                                    2008051525

978-0-307-40918-8

Printed in Singapore

Design by Maureen Erbe/Erbe Design

Additional photographs: Chicago Historical Society (page 63 bottom); Costas Picadas (pages 68 top, 75 right); Matthijs van Roon and Mandy Pieper (pages 92, 93); Michael Moore (page 109 top right); Shane Sigler (page 122, left); Fabian Dominguez (page 199); John B. Murray (page 243 above). Floor plans: Dan Davidson (page 34); Eric J. Smith Architect (page 160); Triarch Architecture (page 206); Denise Rich (page 239)

10  9  8  7  6  5  4  3  2  1

First Edition

**PAGE 2**  To maximize square footage, the owner raised the roof and added two floors to the top of this 19th-century New York building. (See page 200.)

**PAGE 5**  A stellar collection of contemporary photography and late deco and midcentury furnishings almost upstage the unfettered Lake Michigan views in this Chicago high-rise. (See page 102.)

**PAGE 6**  The couple fashioned an utterly unique residence and office space out of a 16,000-square-foot former industrial loft in downtown Los Angeles. (See page 78.)

FOR S.H.D.

# CONTENTS

# INTRODUCTION

From New York to Los Angeles, Miami to Chicago, a new breed of revolutionary urban residents is redefining city living. Forget the sprawling suburban mansion with tennis court and swimming pool—these visionaries are ushering in a golden age of urban utopia right in the heart of the city.

For the first time in history, more of the world's population is living in urban areas than in rural ones—up from just 10 percent in 1900. Demographers estimate that by 2050, 75 percent of us will be living in major metropolitan areas. No doubt about it—we have become an urbanized planet. We are consciously choosing to work, raise our families, and live out our daily existence in sprawling megalopolises—places where space is at a premium and the cost of living can be stratospheric.

Despite the challenges of city living, devoted metropolitan dwellers no longer seem to be fantasizing about inhabiting that big country house or pining for the ease of a more suburban or exurban lifestyle. They value city pleasures more, such as a unique and diverse population, the proximity to cultural and sporting events, better job opportunities, lifestyle variety, and a sense of freedom.

**OPPOSITE** A Calderesque metal light fixture by David Weeks adorns Alex Daly's living room overlooking Biscayne Bay in Miami.

Some also say they are drawn by the intangible "pulse"—the movement and development of ideas, the sense of energy. (The economics writer David Leonhardt probably summed up the trend best when he wrote in the *New York Times*: "Despite all the ways that technology has made distance matter less, geography matters more. It may be easier to transport an individual job from New York to Vermont, but the value of being in New York is actually greater than it used to be.") The "suburbanization" of large cities has also upped the attraction; in New York City, for example, where the number of children under five has increased more than 32 percent since 2000, the Bloomberg administration has cleaned up the air, instituted a smoking ban in public places, and undertaken a parks program so every resident can live within a ten-minute walk of a park by 2030.

The number one thing urbanites say they want (and often lack) is space . . . room . . . square footage. For several years now massive homes have become de rigueur all over the country's suburbs, bedroom communities, and rural areas. Grosse Point, Michigan; Fisher Island, Florida; Jackson Hole, Wyoming; Lake Forest, Illinois . . . even in small towns in Iowa, homes the size of the local mall are ubiquitous. Now, savvy city residents are coming up with innovative ways to carve out larger and larger living spaces for themselves. The people profiled in this book have combined apartments; converted former schools and commercial and industrial properties; even added new floors on top of an old shoe factory built in the 1800s in order to realize their own larger-than-life metropolitan dreams.

I became intrigued with the trend of twenty-first-century urban renewal a year or two ago when I realized that most of my friends and colleagues—including families with four, five, even six children—were staying in the city, be it New York, London, Chicago, or that ready-made megalopolis, Dubai. This is quite a departure from the old pattern of getting married, having a few kids, and immediately decamping for the space, ease, and superior public schools of suburbia.

In some cases, lucky city dwellers have been able to realize the potent dream of not only subsisting in the city, but also of residing there with carte blanche. The people profiled in this book are true urban visionaries. By thinking outside the box, they have completed unique spaces that engage with their environments. Their collective quest to reimagine the metropolitan home and their success in creating a distinct personal urban oasis is fascinating, inspirational, and empowering. Many of those featured took a big gamble on their homes—

**OPPOSITE** Julie and Fred Latsko spent four years painstakingly restoring the historic 16,000-square-foot Dewes mansion in Chicago back to a single-family home.

sinking everything they had into the property years ago or buying in inexpensive fringe areas that had not been gentrified. Through ingenuity, they have been able to accommodate their previously more suburban-friendly interests. In San Francisco, we see how a family created space for their four boys to practice basketball. Unable to build out or up, they ingeniously excavated *under* their Pacific Heights mansion to construct a home court. We find out how Magnus and Karen Walker were able to create a home in LA that could accommodate not only their huge clothing business and his collection of cars, but also areas for hit TV shows to film. Accoutrements such as an indoor/outdoor koi pond, a ballroom, or a private parklike garden where birds alight have been realized in such a seamless way as to appear natural in these unusual settings. So, too, do the everyday rooms, which flow together coherently or play off one another beautifully thanks to the brilliant vision of the residents, the architects, and the designers.

For the owners, the point is not about displaying wealth or increasing real estate value; instead, creating their homes has been a journey in authentically and emotionally connecting with their interests and the chosen cities so close to their hearts.

Aren't we incredibly curious to know who these people are? In what cities they live, what they do for a living, and how they gathered their inspiration to create such idiosyncratic eye-popping spaces? Within these pages, we'll discover how a single person, like Dan Davidson, utilizes 17,000 square feet of living space (a former synagogue, no less) in Miami. Chicagoans Fred and Julie Latsko reveal how they acquired and renovated a 16,000-square-foot landmarked limestone mansion from the 1800s, turning it into a comfortable and modern family home. We'll learn how world-famous artist Izhar Patkin and a few friends transformed an old vocational school into sprawling condominiums in the heart of New York City. The following pages take you behind the scenes in these modern-day metropolitan Hearst Castles, revealing the personal stories and secrets from the often notoriously private owners, innovative architects, and celebrated designers. These experienced professionals and residents impart ideas and knowledge for anyone thinking about creating his or her own urban fantasy escape. This book is the delicious answer to the perennial question, How would I live in the city if there were no limits?

**OPPOSITE** Originally a coal truck depot, this Greenwich Village townhouse is now a contemporary family home featuring an oxidized metal skylight cut into the terrace above.

"Begin with the end in mind." Simple advice to follow, when baking a cake or giving a speech. But only those with incredible vision and even more courage could apply that concept when converting a dilapidated 28,000-square-foot New York City building into a dream home. Again . . . that's 28,000 square feet. In New York City.

Walking down the popular Tribeca street where the building sits, it is hard to imagine that the distinguished and immaculate stucco structure was ever abandoned or in disrepair. "I used to walk the dog with a list of available buildings," says the owner, who eventually bought the building with her husband. "When I saw this one in late 2000, it was boarded up and the first floor was completely covered, but you could see it was still beautiful." Tired of living under the rules and regulations of co-ops and wanting more room for themselves, their three children, and their dog, the family looked for a vacant building for more than six years. (The owners succinctly describe this period as "Look . . . get disappointed . . . renovate current apartment . . . look . . . get disappointed . . . buy new apartment . . . look. . . .") Though they had no definitive size requirement, they knew they needed something wide—wide enough to accommodate the large scale of their art collection.

**OPPOSITE** Joe Jaroff created the brilliant suspended glass staircase, topped off with a skylight that seemingly electrifies each step and transfers natural brightness to every floor.

Most New York City townhouses run on average anywhere from 18 to 23 feet in width. But this place (in what has become one of the most popular and expensive neighborhoods in the city) was different—namely, it was a building, not a house, so it was a princely 40 feet wide, 100 feet deep, and eight stories tall (including six aboveground, one basement, and one subbasement).

Built around 1859, the structure was one of a group of three original buildings that were used as dry goods department stores, later becoming a wholesale shoe warehouse. The couple were first shown the property in the fall of 2000 and quickly made it theirs. They began renovation in August of 2001, and then on September 11 the Twin Towers fell just a few blocks south, halting work for four months of the nearly three-year project. "Every single thing you can think of needed work," remembers the wife. "A new sewer line to the street, creating a gas line that never existed, replacing the back wall on the lower floors that had basically fallen off, placing steel beams under the sidewalk, restoring the interior brick, and raising the roof, to name just a few projects." Most complicated, though, might have been restoring the façade of the building, as most of North Tribeca has been landmarked since 1992. (New York City's Landmarks Preservation Commission seeks to protect those neighborhoods with historically significant architecture, ensuring that there is continuity in materials, texture, and lines when a building is being renovated. This mandate can generate what some perceive to be creative limitations.) These owners endured the accompanying customary years of paperwork and logistics, using the building's history almost as a guide or course of action. "We would never do anything other than a restoration," says the wife. "The building exists as a permanent historical structure—we are just visiting."

**LEFT** The fourth-floor gallery provides a gracious public area separating the master suite, children's bedrooms, and laundry area. An Andrew Polk painting adds a jolt of orange and saffron. Joe Jaroff custom made the beautiful vitrine on the left.

This philosophy clearly informed their design scheme, which can be summed up in one word: *temporary*. The part Boffi, part custom-made stainless-steel kitchen is not traditionally "built in"—it stands on legs with open shelves and could be easily disassembled and moved. The Daniel Romualdez–designed bookcases also have legs and no backs. The lighting, air-conditioning, and even the staircase are hung by wires. "We can just cut the wires, pick up our stuff, and go," says the wife. "The building existed before us, and with our work and hope, it will live on after us."

In the end the owners did divide up some of the immense space, leasing to retail on the street level and renting out a few apartments on the second and third floors. As the final product reveals, the couple clearly didn't need the entire building to make their grand statement. Stepping out of the elevator into the family's home, which occupies the top three floors (and basement), can only be described as utterly mind-blowing. A transcendent suspended glass and metal staircase, topped off with a skylight, immediately grabs attention, anchoring the space in an unparalleled way. Joe Jaroff of Mison Concepts has made a bold, dazzling, and completely contemporary statement (and achieved a "major engineering feat" according to the owners); the staircase updates the historic building with a funky urban gloss. (It was also an ingenious way to transfer light to all three floors.) The 14-foot ceilings, effervescent interiors, and jolts of color on the walls make the space feel electric. On the top floor sits a seductive lounge–cum–game room, complete with pool table and baby grand piano. Light floods this entire floor from a skylight along the front and a wall of gorgeous gridlike stainless-steel windows along the back, which lead to a spectacular rooftop terrace. Patricia McCobb—who is

**RIGHT** Sleek stainless-steel Boffi cabinetry and counters, juxtaposed against the original brick wall from the 1800s, give the kitchen a luxe contemporary update. Putnam Ladder Company makes the rolling ladder. A skylight bathes the space in natural illumination.

The massive main living floor is spectacularly dramatic, with 14-foot ceilings, pulsating cherry red perimeter walls, and no dividing walls (instead, a standing bookcase at far back left separates the library from a generous office/family computer room). A fresh white upholstered sofa and chairs came from ABC Carpet and are paired with an elegant Indian daybed. Two oversized works on paper by Doug and Mike Starn hang on the brick wall.

responsible for the renovation of the Great Lawn in Central Park—designed a charming city escape, full of planted boxes, seating areas, and intricate irrigation.

The seductive soul of the home is the main living level. Everywhere one looks are flawless examples of work that a group of superstar artisans contributed to the home. Architect Mario Rivelli is responsible for the gracious layout and constructed the fireplace Daniel Romualdez designed to seamlessly accompany the original brick. All of the wood floors were lifted, planed, and replaced by Norwegian Wood, then stained a very specific mix of brown/black by John Pomiankowski. "We went to a stable in Montauk, so I could show him a horse whose depth of color I wanted to match," remembers the wife.

The lowest level contains all of the private rooms, including a jaw-dropping master suite. Its accompanying bath is a lavishly sexy wraparound affair with several different areas and cowhide rugs. Though surely the grandest design gesture of all for an urban residence is the subterranean basketball court (with 17-foot ceilings) and mezzanine gym that the couple created out of what was originally two basement levels, where the children have entertained their entire school classes.

Supporting the floors in a building of this size and age is a feat in and of itself. Luckily the structure was one of the first of its time to be made with steel beams, which are, unbelievably, close to 18 inches thick. "When we cut out the opening to build the stairs," remembers the husband, "we were shocked to find that it was already framed by steel girders." Rumor has it that the building originally had a center courtyard, currently where the stairs reside. "This made our job of securing the staircase much easier," he adds. An additional difficulty with many large homes is concealing the enormous amount of mechanical elements that it takes to power the space—something this family wanted to ensure did not visually interfere with the design. To achieve this goal, they dropped ceilings only in

closets to hide air handlers and ductwork. "You should know that our architect and AC contractor thought we were insane for being so demanding in this regard," chuckles the husband.

Visitors must wonder if having so much space in New York City makes it an easier place to live, a better place to live, than the suburbs. Or simply what it's like for just one family to live in such a large home. "Yes . . . it's nicer," laughs the wife. "And yes, everyone comments. I think more people are staying in the city as a basic economic fact—we've moved from a city of renters to a city of owners, which makes it harder to move. And personally, we can't see the appeal of the suburbs." It's no wonder.

**ABOVE** The original building included two basement levels, which the owners combined to create a basketball court, a mezzanine gym, and two locker rooms.

**OPPOSITE, ABOVE** A cool metal-ball-beaded curtain conceals one of the children's rooms, decked out in a zebra-print rug. The bright red walls and ocean blue chair lend energy to the space.

**OPPOSITE, BELOW** Award-winning landscape architect Patricia McCobb designed an urban oasis of boxed plantings that surround the rooftop retreat. Comfortable teak and upholstered furnishings from Kinsgley-Bate are sprinkled throughout the vast deck, offering stellar views of New York City from every seat.

**ABOVE** An oasis of calm and serenity, the master bath features muted Calcutta marble counters and floor tiles from Urban Archaeology. All fixtures are Waterworks, and the cowhide rug was found at the El Paso Trading Company.

**RIGHT** The owner's use of epic skylights as well as side lot-line windows along the far wall of the top floor was a clever design solution to ensure the old dry goods department store would draw in plenty of light. A white Mies van der Rohe leather Barcelona lounger can be seen in the left foreground; an antique Steinway grand piano is in the background.

The enormous top floor has a glossy, cool boutique-hotel vibe. Norwegian Wood added the gleaming wood ceiling that almost seems like a contemporary nod to modern master Richard Neutra. The B&B Italia white sofa and a pair of iconic Barcelona chairs pop against the nearly black stained floors and ceiling.

# TEMPLE HOUSE

As savvy urban homeowners look for innovative ways to create larger and larger living spaces, the conversion of former commercial or industrial properties into over-the-top residences is skyrocketing. Former schools, YMCAs, and factories have been turned into homes all over the country—though usually with multiple apartments. In Dan Davidson's case, what was once an Orthodox synagogue with more than a thousand members has become his very own private eye-popping abode in Miami's über-hip South Beach neighborhood.

Only a truly bold and clever real estate investor would envision a Zen Balinese–inspired home after seeing the dilapidated Kneseth Israel Congregation building in 2003. Originally designed in 1933 by well-known art deco architect and native Floridian L. Murray Dixon as a single-family home, the structure was in great disrepair when Davidson happened on the building in a rainstorm, just as the "for sale" sign was being staked in the ground. Davidson had fled New York City for the safety and warmth of south Miami right after 9/11, planning to stay just a few days. Those days turned into weeks and then into months, until finally he realized he was never going to leave . . . so he purchased the property and embarked on a wild, nearly three-year-long renovation odyssey.

**LEFT** A view of the congregants' seats before the temple was converted back into a single-family home.

**OPPOSITE** Davidson plays with shapes and materials to create the perfect whimsical party pad with understated glamour. Geometrical teak and white canvas chairs surround cocktail tables, arranged in intimate seating areas.

The mammoth great room does feel a bit like an airplane hangar, albeit a completely contemporary and New Age one. Everything in the home is a reflection of Davidson's personality and life: white leather sofas of his design flank a low-slung wood cocktail table, behind which hangs a pure gold and silver painting on canvas also created by him.

The original bones of the two-story structure—which had been converted to a synagogue in 1942—were definitely worth saving: Dixon was famous for his pioneering work that helped make Miami Beach the unofficial capital of art deco design. (There are more art deco buildings in Miami Beach than anywhere else in the world.) Many of Dixon's enduring and distinctive designs still dot the current landscape—the Raleigh Hotel (1940), the Marlin (1939), and the Tides Hotel (1936) being popular examples. The synagogue building had been granted historic landmark status years before Davidson purchased it, which precluded any changes to the façade, but he quickly got to work on everything else—most daringly without a proper architect or interior designer.

"I'm an entrepreneur, primarily in biotech and now Internet businesses, and when I bought the place I was simply naïve. I had no idea what I was doing—I thought it would be a three-month process! But then I had to get permits, variances, have the building rezoned . . . and ended up working closely with City Hall. My contractor, L. P. Cook, became indispensable and was a real partner in the project," Davidson says. Preservationists will appreciate the painstaking lengths that he went to in preserving and restoring historically important details. The curve of the roof, the original windows, the balcony where congregants sat during services . . . all have been lovingly refurbished. Even the replication of something as seemingly

**OPPOSITE** Classic art deco curves are the creation of pioneering architect L. Murray Dixon, who designed the home in 1933. The structure was converted to a synagogue in 1942. A wood bench with suede cushions from Eclectic Elements stands against the far wall.

**ABOVE LEFT** Dan Davidson at home.

**ABOVE RIGHT** Tall hedges of ficus and palms partially obscure the art deco historic landmark structure—the largest single-family home in the South Beach area of Miami.

**LEFT** A serious home in sunny South Florida would not be complete without a serious terrace. Palm trees and simple Hampton Bays woven teak furniture dot the Brazilian ipe wood deck, creating a perfect outdoor living room.

**BELOW** An architectural rendering of the home's gargantuan first floor.

**OPPOSITE** A view from the former bimah (altar) where the rabbi would speak to his congregation. Elegant white leather and stainless-steel sofas designed by Davidson and manufactured by McKinley Pierre Furniture meld with the airy surroundings and strike an overall feeling of an avant-garde beach home with a Balinese twist. Davidson also designed the floating glass and metal railing that snakes along the edge of the balcony.

inconsequential as the original concrete floor was meticulously handled: Davidson had an entire new floor poured, and because of its size, cement trucks had to line up around the block so each could access the building at various locations with hoses and pour at the same time. He then added a high-gloss finish that gives the surface a surreal liquid appearance.

Guests enter through a long hallway (lined by a mini screening room, a guest room, and his-and-hers industrial-sized bathrooms), pull back gossamer white drapes, and suddenly step into the mind-blowing main room, with a 25-foot-high ceiling. (Also on this ground-floor level is the monstrous loft.) Staircases flank either side of the balcony and lead upstairs to a labyrinth of private rooms—including the master suite, guest suites, and the substantial kitchen. Placing the kitchen on the second floor makes perfect sense once visitors realize this location provides direct access to the expansive outdoor deck.

The décor of the colossal 16,350-square-foot home—now the largest single-family home in all of South Beach and one which

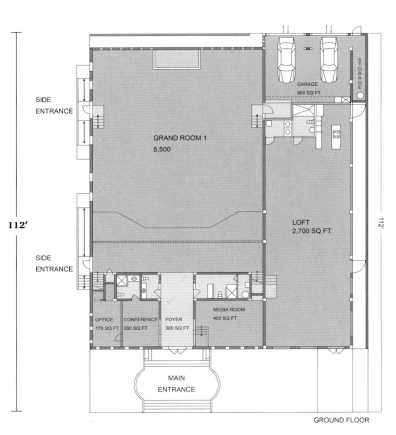

sits on two adjacent lots—has a groovy Asian vibe that is striking and unexpected. The refreshing aesthetic creates a modern space using a classic art deco backdrop. Custom-made white leather sofas, daybeds imported from Bali and outfitted with flowing gauzy material, and Buddha heads give the home a feeling of calm and comfort . . . an oasis from the outside world. Often, large spaces, particularly with deco architecture, can be a bit cold, so Davidson's choice of softer furnishings provides some critical balance, especially in the epic main room. The sunlight that streams through this area also adds a rather mystical sensation.

"Though I didn't use an interior designer, I did have the help of a good friend, Monica Seleske, who owns a local design showroom, Eclectic Elements." Through Monica, Davidson found pieces such as the sharp, rectangular mahogany and white leather chairs, low-slung cocktail tables, and cow-print rugs that adorn the balcony. A decidedly more casual design scheme is found on the oversized deck—a luxurious outdoor

living room that only homeowners in the warmer climes can fully enjoy. This second-story terrace (just off the kitchen), outfitted with barbecues, luscious landscaping, and even mini palm trees, is the area in the home that most aptly and genuinely reflects the laid-back sun, surf, and sand attitude for which South Beach has become world renowned. The kitchen itself is simple marble and stainless steel, with an inviting long oak dining table that ups the coziness factor.

Without a doubt, this is a pad any bachelor would envy (especially considering the Jacuzzi in the living room). One can't help but wonder, though, if Davidson ever gets just a little bit lonely, rattling around in a house with four bedrooms, four bathrooms, a professional-grade kitchen, a screening room, and an enormous office (not to mention that airport hangar–like living room) all by himself. "No—I spend so much time in my office, the kitchen, and my bedroom that it doesn't seem that large most of the time," Davidson says. "And it's not that I was specifically *looking* for such a large home—I just found a

Light from three sides drenches the professional-grade GE Monogram kitchen. Davidson loves to throw dinner parties for eighteen to twenty people—all of whom can fit at the extra-long wood table brought back from India. The granite countertops are by LPC, and the statue was purchased in Phuket, Thailand.

property that happened to inspire me." He adds, "I'm lucky too because I also entertain quite a bit. . . . I love throwing dinner parties for eighteen to twenty friends." This is clearly one serious party venue: Davidson has hosted events for the likes of Al Gore, the Miami Symphony, and J.Lo.

Though it seems like more of a human characteristic, there *is* a palpable joie de vivre that seems to emanate from the house. Maybe it's the energy of being in the center of the action: the shopping and nightlife meccas Lincoln Road and Collins Avenue sit just a few blocks away. Or maybe it's the home's proximity to the Miami Convention Center, where the legendary fabulosity of Art Basel takes place each year. Davidson seems to have drawn on all of these elements to create this special place, while also resurrecting an architectural masterpiece.

**ABOVE**  An office adjacent the entry was turned into a small home theater, complete with two rows of stuffed leather chairs and a maple Ido daybed for lounging, all from Eclectic Elements.

**LEFT**  It's hard to imagine what the synagogue's former congregants would think of Davidson's conversion to a slick bachelor pad. The master bedroom is awash in white leather sofas and white walls. The cowhide rug and deep pile shag carpet add texture.

# PALAZZO IN THE SKY

There are people who painstakingly look for the perfect home for years and then there are those lucky enough just to happen upon a space and say, "I'll take it" . . . all the more improbable when said space is one of the largest condos on the market in South Florida. Several years ago an elegant Miami couple was preparing to purchase a (standard-size) unit at the Ritz-Carlton in Coconut Grove. "Audrey Ross, the venerable Christie's real estate agent, just wanted to show us the views here," the British-born wife remembers about the grand home. "We walked in and my husband suddenly said it needed to be his. We honestly didn't plan on buying such an immense space—it was just the views . . . but I do love that it feels like being in a house."

**LEFT** The skyline of downtown Miami can be seen from the kitchen. A midcentury glass-top table is paired with wood and stainless-steel chairs.

**OPPOSITE** Sunlight floods the comfortable and airy top-floor pool room, where designer Kevin Gray did his "diva design touches." He continued the soft caramel shades of the unhoned travertine floors in the handsome furnishings, including the Donghia Block Island club sofa and club chairs upholstered in a soft cream Glant chenille. He added a dash of personal flair with pieces he custom designed: the chocolate leather ottoman with Lucite feet and a pair of round side tables in smoked and clear Lucite.

**ABOVE** No need to take the elevator down to the building pool—the couple has their own, fifty stories in the sky.

**RIGHT** The oak and glass staircase and balcony connect the upper wings of the home. A custom Kevin Gray Designs sofa upholstered in Bellaqua velvet sits in the foreground. The walls are covered with the owners' contemporary Cuban art collection.

**ABOVE** Expansive hallways connect the various wings of the vast apartment. A French antique daybed with silk leopard pillows and various African masks and sculptures from Mali and Burkina Faso greet visitors at the entry hall.

**OPPOSITE** The staggering double-height vista looking east over shimmering Biscayne Bay and one of the many terraces. A pale knotted geometric-patterned Skala wool carpet from Stark shines under an antique Chinese coffee table.

Mention Brickell Avenue—the boulevard on which the couple lives—to almost anyone in Miami and lots of "oohs" and "aahs" inevitably tumble forth, along with descriptions like "superluxurious" and "most desirable area in Miami." The couple's building and swank Brickell Avenue sit right on Biscayne Bay—some of the primest of prime waterfront property around (residents can dock their boats at the private marina outside their back door). At fifty-two stories, the building was the tallest residential development south of New York City at the time it was built. Internationally acclaimed architect Luis Revuelta's dramatic design, coupled with lush landscaping—gumbo limbo trees, tropical gardens, cascading waterfalls, hammocks and gazebos—and the stunning bay vistas make the building feel much more like an idyllic island oasis than your basic urban high-rise.

But the crown jewel of the building, to be sure, is the 16,000-square-foot triplex penthouse apartment, comprising 11,700 square feet of interior space and 4,300 square feet of exterior terrace. The owners, a financial analyst and his philanthropist wife, brought in celebrated interior designer Kevin Gray to oversee the massive job of selecting and placing furnishings. "I went to tour the apartment," Kevin recalls, "and the rooms were so vast! Three floors and a main room larger than the *piano nobile* of a palazzo on the Grand Canal. But here we were on the fiftieth floor looking out over the world. The rooms were overpowering, and the glass and views just went on forever. So, my task became, How do I turn this airplane hangar into the Concorde lounge, with the client's own touch and as a comfortable home?"

The views are absolutely, utterly heart-stopping, seemingly unparalleled in a private home. On multiple levels, terraces wrap around *one half of the entire building,* featuring limitless vistas of Biscayne Bay, Coral Gables, and the twinkling lights of the Miami skyline. "The nights are amazing—to sit outside . . . the lights . . . it's just magical," say the owners, who have two grown children. "We have a Fourth of July party every year and from up here you can see the fireworks going off in Fort Lauderdale and all the way down in Key West." On the top floor of the apartment a hallway leads to a modern and playful "pool room," and then *boom*—one walks right onto the most vast and dramatic of all of the terraces and a pool, 500 feet in the sky. The sun, wind, view, and especially the elevation create an overwhelming, almost intoxicating (and slightly terrifying) sensation. This was designer Gray's favorite area to work with. "The upstairs triple-high top floor, the terrace, the pool—it's all about entertaining, and is where I did my diva touch," he states. "Many of the furnishings on that floor actually came from my old penthouse in Miami Beach and from Donghia," the designer says. In order to protect the art collection, prevent the furnishings from fading, and keep the notorious Miami sun from heating up the apartment, the couple installed motorized solar-mesh window treatments on all of the dozens of windows, which were already chemically tinted. They then installed hurricane shutters throughout "for the price of three Ferraris!" winces the wife.

Gray sought design inspiration for the interiors from the worldly couple and from one of their great passions: Cuban art. (As most people know by now, Miami has experienced a significant cultural renaissance over the last five to ten years—aided by arguably the most influential art fair in the world, Art Basel Miami Beach, which has produced a vibrant and cutting-edge arts and design community.) The discreet couple has amassed

**LEFT** A wide view of the immense pool room. The pair of glass lamps with brown mesh raffia shades are vintage.

an eclectic collection of primarily contemporary Cuban pieces with a Caribbean flair that infuses the space with color and romance. Gray's furnishings juxtapose nicely with some of the exotic art. "The fabrics I chose needed to work with their collection, the existing flooring, and Venetian plaster walls," says Gray. "The owner loves color and contrasts." Furnishings were brought in from the clients' homes in London, Paris, and New York City, and many items were transformed to fit the space. "Things had to be raised and extended with custom wood feet to work with the high ceilings and the huge space. Paintings were grouped or hung separately or even placed over landings and above doorways! It was a process of getting to know the clients and then pulling each piece together over a year." The result is the ultimate twenty-first-century home that epitomizes life in South Florida for an international family. The most charming decorative element is the family photos. Pictures of the kids skiing, laughing, and graduating from school line several hallways, filling the apartment with an aura of happiness and confirming that love is the most important accessory in this home.

When asked what the best thing is about having seven bedrooms, seven full bathrooms, two half baths, and one pool shower room, the wife laughs. "Well, the terraces are lovely. And it's so nice not to have to worry about a lawn, the sprinklers. . . It's fantastic that when something breaks, the building staff fixes it, and they carry my luggage up!" Even with all of this space, it's still the small things in life that matter.

**ABOVE**  In addition to its spectacular view, the large dining room features a George III mahogany table and twelve Regency-era chairs. An art deco chandelier hangs above the table, which rests on an antique Persian rug.

**OPPOSITE**  "We had fun with fabrics," says designer Kevin Gray. "The owner has a very keen sense of color." Various shades of blue were used to play off the ever-changing color of the Miami sky. The upholstered sofa was found in Paris.

**ABOVE** Fifty stories in the sky, stone pillars and a gazebo partially shade the expansive terrace facing south toward Coconut Grove and Coral Gables.

## WHEN THE BALLROOM BECOMES THE BEDROOM

Some people are drawn to modern homes. Others prefer brick Georgian or Craftsman. Fred and Julie Latsko seem to gravitate toward homes with significant history and an interesting backstory. A few years ago the Chicago couple purchased Oprah's 160-acre Indiana farm as a weekend retreat for themselves and their young daughter. The property includes a 9,700-square-foot French-style château, a guesthouse, a pool, stables, an orchard, a tennis court, and a helicopter pad. That's big. And, if Oprah owned it and was entertaining buddies like Julia Roberts and Tina Turner there, it naturally follows that it must be phenomenal. With a spread like that, a tiny two-bedroom city apartment might suffice for some.

Not so for this family. Fred, a real estate developer, and Julie, an interior designer and partner (with Oprah's chef, Art Smith, no less) in the wildly popular Chicago restaurant Table 52, recently completed renovating the historic Dewes Mansion back into a single-family home. Originally built sometime between 1894 and 1896 by beer tycoon Francis J. Dewes, the German baroque and French rococo architecture–style home sits on a huge corner lot in downtown Chicago's fashionable Lincoln Park neighborhood, just a few blocks from the lake. The mansion created quite a stir upon completion, as Dewes had built a home that rivaled the palaces of Europe.

**OPPOSITE** Beer magnet Francis J. Dewes built the mansion between 1894 and 1896 in what is now one of Chicago's toniest lakefront neighborhoods. The majestic architecture is a mix of baroque, French rococo, and art nouveau, and when built was comparable to the size and luxury of European palaces.

**ABOVE** Gorgeous restored pocket doors open from the main entrance hall into the living room. A nineteenth-century François Linke desk sits in the window nook.

**RIGHT** The expansive master suite encompasses the home's entire top floor, formerly the ballrom that sat 120 for dinner. The owners added a glamorous La Murrina chandelier. The bed is by Karges, next to a nineteenth-century French Empire armoire.

With its limestone façade, intricate eighteenth-century rococo ornamentation, opulent interior (the Gothic library was supposedly imported from a European castle), and starchitect pedigree (Cudell and Hercz), the structure reportedly cost a whopping $200,000 to build—at a time when the average home price was around $2,100.

The home changed hands several times over the years; one of its most memorable incarnations was as a wedding location in the 1980s and '90 s, when the ballroom alone could seat 120 for dinner. It was during this time that the property caught the eye of her husband, remembers Julie. "Fred had been to the mansion for a party and always had a dream of making it into a single-family home. One day it came on the market, and here we are." The couple was drawn not only to the home's unique nature and historical significance but also to the opportunity to remain living downtown. "We really wanted to raise our children in the city," Julie says. "The suburbs never seemed to be an option with work and our love of diversity, people, and excitement. Chicago is such a family-friendly city, too—most of our friends now opt to stay downtown and raise their kids."

The couple had no idea, though, that staying in the city would require so much work. They acquired the Dewes Mansion in 2004 and worked tirelessly for four years to renovate the landmarked beauty (both the exterior and, unusually, parts of the interior are on the historic preservation list). As their intention was always to restore the home to its original grandeur, Julie delved into the background of the property, conducting research at the Chicago Historical Society and exploring ways to refurbish many of the existing lavish original elements, such as the two-story painted-glass window, a jaw-dropping wishing well with life-sized

**LEFT** In the astonishing formal entry, the Latskos restored the exquisite mosaic tile floor back to its original luster. The gleaming Scagliola marble walls, pillars, plasterwork, and moldings are also from the 1890s. Shown at the Chicago World's Fair in 1893, the detailed ironwork on the main staircase won several awards and was installed in the home soon after.

marble figures, and various light fixtures. "The good news was that not much had been touched or removed from the home since the Deweses had lived there," Julie offers. Then again, the fact that not much had been touched meant that more than a hundred years of grime needed to be removed . . . plumbing and electrical systems updated . . . wood and tile floors refurbished. Luckily the couple was able to restore hardware and light fixtures that were unique to each room and to clean up the ironwork on the grand staircase—ironwork that had won many accolades in the Chicago World's Fair in 1893 (also known as the Columbian World's Fair) before it was installed in the house. Certainly some of the most fabulous original outré accoutrements that remain are the male and female stone figures that greet visitors at the front door—a sly prelude to what is to come inside.

And, *comme c'est magnifique*! The interiors are breathtaking. "The home was modeled after Versailles," continues Julie, "so I also got inspiration from that." For several years she searched auctions all over the world to find period-perfect furnishings to fill the 16,000-square-foot, six-bedroom, nine-bathroom home. "The design scheme was to keep the interiors fitting with the

**TOP LEFT**  Below gilded moldings in the first-floor entry hall, a life-sized marble wishing well with sculptures of lovers and a small Cupid welcomes visitors.

**LEFT**  Heavily toiled leather walls adorn the gothic library, reportedly imported from an old European castle. An opulent light fixture illuminates antique chairs upholstered in fabric from Old World Weavers that sit on a carpet by Stark.

**OPPOSITE**  The owners had years of dirt and buildup removed from an eye-popping two-story painted-glass window of historical significance; it is now a central focal point of the home.

**ABOVE** Current owners Fred and Julie Latsko purchased the historic property in 2004 and spent four painstaking years restoring the home to its original grandeur. Behind the couple sculptures carved out of limestone flank the front door, supporting the balcony on the second floor.

**RIGHT** Color and pattern fill a cheerful guest room. Latsko mixed a Stark carpet with Scalamandré fabric wallcoverings, drapes, and bed linens. The early nineteenth-century Louis XV salon suite was purchased at auction.

style of the home," Julie elaborates, "but warm everything up." Scalamandré fabrics and bright colors soften the crisp symmetry of the classical European architecture and the ornate details.

On the ground-floor level are several living rooms, the dining room, a completely new kitchen, and the über-grand main staircase. The second floor is full of guest rooms and the daughter's suite. The most visually arresting area by far is the master suite, spread over the entire top floor of the home. Originally designed as a Louis XVI ballroom, it has been transformed into private rooms fit for, well . . . a king. A gymnasium-sized bedroom, his-and-hers baths, two rooms converted into custom closets, and a nursery exude the feel of a luxurious English country house. Only the lower level has a contemporary atmosphere, with a kids' theater, a bar, and billiards.

For a couple that clearly likes to make a large residential statement, the Latskos are also known around town for being low-key, unpretentious, and family-centric. "The greatest advantage to having so much space downtown is that we won't ever have to move again!" laughs Julie. "We can raise our family and entertain our friends all in the same place. And we have plenty of space to grow."

**OPPOSITE** The gracious second-floor landing leads to several guest rooms and the daughter's suite. A nineteenth-century commode is paired with upholstered Louis XV chairs.

**ABOVE LEFT** Architects Adolph Cudell and Arthur Hercz used imported French oak paneling to create built-in credenzas and an elaborate coffered ceiling in the formal dining room. An original light fixture hangs above a custom-designed table, complemented by fine Ebanista chairs covered in Scalamandré fabric.

**LEFT** A photo of the home, circa 1900.

Custom-made wall coverings and window treatments by Old World Weavers lend a completely authentic air to the lavish conservatory. Several Louis XV chairs, covered in decorative eighteenth-century Scalamandré fabric, are paired with an immaculate tall case clock from the same period. Original wall sconces, French rococo ornaments, and gilded moldings were restored to perfection.

# A CHARITABLE HISTORY

In 1919, the wildly successful financier and philanthropist Jeremiah Milbank donated his extraordinary New York City home to the Ladies' Christian Union. A lifelong believer in volunteerism, Milbank gave a fortune to charity and helped change the lives of many. His colossal "Milbank House," in the heart of Greenwich Village, was transformed into a boarding residence, providing safe and affordable housing to young women studying or working in the city. Originally built in 1847, the astonishing 55-foot-wide, 5-story building included 31 bedrooms and gave critical assistance to thousands of women until 1996, when it was sold to New York University, passing hands again in 2000 to a private owner.

Finally, in 2007, fate seems to have intervened and the home found owners who share Milbank's charitable mission of helping others. "You know, we weren't really looking for this house; it found us," remembers the wife. "We'd outgrown our former space of 1,600 square feet, but we didn't want to leave the neighborhood after living here since 1993."

**LEFT** Built in 1847, the 55-foot-wide home in New York's Greenwich Village was donated by philanthropist Jeremiah Milbank to the Ladies' Christian Union, which constructed thirty-one bedrooms and used it as a boardinghouse. The current owners acquired the property in 2007.

**OPPOSITE** Looking from a sitting room into the dining room, the massive depth of the home becomes apparent. Aspiring pianists and composers can often be found at the Steinway grand piano, circa 1907.

The couple, an actress turned film producer/theater director and her husband—ironically, a financial executive turned philanthropist—use the extensive space for a myriad of altruistic, humanitarian, intellectual, and artistic interests. "The large space is really for entertaining and raising money for the charities that we are involved in," the wife offers. Indeed, special lighting was installed for presentations, speeches, and readings for groups close to their hearts, primarily in education, theater, and music. "My favorite thing about having the space is feeling that there is room for people to exchange ideas, play music, make art, converse, and laugh," she says. "Concert pianists and young composers come create and practice. The house is just always somehow filled with people, kids, even dogs!"

The owners undertook a complete gut renovation of the property, hiring David Piscuskas and his firm, 1100 Architect. Piscuskas has been art-world royalty's designer of choice for years (Jasper Johns, Brice Marden, Eric Fischl and April Gornick, David Salle, and Ross Bleckner are reportedly all residential clients). Interestingly, Piscuskas was the architect who handled the conversion of the space back to a single-family home for the client who purchased the property in 2000. "His firm had

**ABOVE LEFT**  The enormity of the home is evident when viewed from the back garden.

**LEFT**  A wall of floor-to-ceiling windows infuses the formal dining room with natural light and provides stunning views of the garden one story below. Various lanterns found in London antiques shops hang over the exquisite custom-made rosewood table, surrounded by chairs upholstered in velvet.

**OPPOSITE**  A soaring double-height library–cum–game room exudes a playful sophistication. All of the millwork, including the zebrawood shelving and parchment doors, was custom made by Nick Mongiardo of Decorative Arts. The floor is walnut.

an aborted chance at the former renovation," says the wife. "It was fun to see them get to complete their work." And complete it they did. A collection of interconnected rooms with an old-world feeling and soaring ceilings wraps around a 1,700-square-foot garden enclosed in stained teak fencing. On every level, a wall of towering windows infuses the home with sunlight and provides views of the delightful backyard (transformed from what had been a basketball court). The authenticity of the double-wide brick mid-1800s architecture and the room proportions remains, but with a sexed-up modern gloss now. The spaces—like the extraordinary double-height zebrawood library—are not only visually splendid and rich but also functional.

The owners turned to good friend and longtime collaborator Bryan Kollman (who has designed both residential and commercial spaces for the couple) to create the dazzling interiors and strike a balance between the clients' eclectic style and the modern architectural palette of 1100 Architect. Kollman's early costume work for the stage, film, and ballet is evident in the theatricality of the space. "There is that thread of drama in the home because so many of us working on the project, including the lighting designer, are from the theater," says Kollman. From the zebra-print runner that winds its way up the seemingly endless staircase to the shagreen sharkskin bar top or the mishmash of lanterns that hang in the formal dining room, the space feels one part adventure, one part performance. To keep things distinctive, much of the furniture was custom made, such as the exquisite 18-foot rosewood dining table and a bronze cast Rateau-esque bird table in the master bedroom. "We were inspired by art deco, art nouveau, and the arts and crafts

**LEFT** A music room with its original walnut floors leads into one of several chic sitting rooms on the first floor. The painting depicting acrobats on the far right wall is by Moreno Pincas.

The firm 1100 Architect designed the modern staircase that
snakes up the home's five flights. Kollman added the dynamic
custom zebra-print wool and cut-pile runner by Stark.

**LEFT** Two round glass-topped tables are paired with a celadon Coolhouse sofa in a front lounge. Emily Todhunter crystal Seapod sconces hang on the wall above.

**ABOVE** Both the formal dining room above and the casual breakfast room below look out on the verdant garden of hydrangeas, ferns, and Japanese toad lilies.

periods," says Kollman. "The owners and I strived to create a harmonious balance of elements from those eras in the overall design." The client adds, "We also wanted the design to be playful and feminine."

Another resolution they had was to build as thoughtfully and ecologically as possible. "It became a sort of game to figure out how we could make it as green as we could—how to recycle, renew, and reinvent," offers the wife. "For example, to use recycled blue jeans for insulation is a great idea, but how green is it to dump the old fiberglass in the landfill? We ended up using both." LED lighting, low VOC paints, earth-friendly finishes, and recycled wood were also employed.

Mother Nature herself had a hand in this property as well: the verdant and enchanting garden. Famed landscape architect Maggie Condon and gardener Kai Hinkaty's lush handiwork includes a rambling mix of hydrangeas, red-bark maple, hemlock, ferns, and Japanese toad lilies, interspersed with a path of limestone pavers. "We have dinners out there in the spring and summer, bird-watch, and keep an eye on the marauding neighborhood cats," laughs the wife. A gardening devotee, she can also indulge her passion in the rooftop green-house, used for wintering plants and teatime escapes.

Even with all of the divine outdoor space, one wonders if the couple ever gets the itch to flee the megalopolis. "It's easy to feel confined in the city," says the wife. "But with this home we are able to relax, unwind, and escape the hustle and bustle. Plus, the people we know who have left the city all want to come back—they miss the tempo, the culture, the creativity, and the diversity of experience. It's New York City, for heaven's sake!"

**RIGHT** The most formal sitting room exudes a definitively French deco tone. Kollman had Madeline Weinrib of ABC Carpet custom make the silk and wool rug, based on a similar Jacques-Émile Ruhlmann design, on which sits a sleek André Arbus daybed. Against the far left wall is a classic Ruhlmann *secrétaire* from Holly Johnson.

# ALL THE HOME IS A STAGE

There is over-the-top . . . and then there is the LA version of over-the-top. It somehow seems fitting that the city that is home to the world's most infamous playboy, Hugh Hefner, and the world's most successful television show ever, *Baywatch*, and the "happiest place on earth," Disneyland (according to their website), would produce the largest apartment in this book.

What on earth does one do with 26,000 square feet of space that is one's own personal home sweet home? Building almost six NBA basketball courts is one option. Installing three Olympic-sized pools is another. Magnus and Karen Walker chose a third, turning a gritty old industrial warehouse into a wild giant mod retro '60s-meets-goth dream loft. "Of course we didn't need a building this size," says Magnus, "yet when the opportunity presented itself, we took advantage. Our friends definitely thought we were crazy."

**LEFT** The exterior of the warehouse, originally built in 1906, belies the imaginative world the couple has created inside.

**OPPOSITE** Funky maximalism reigns in iridescent shapes. A '70s light fixture found at the Rose Bowl Flea Market mixes with a stainless-steel lamp made of silver balls. A pair of tin stars custom made for Serious Clothing retail stores leans against the brick wall next to a tall metallic wall fixture left over from a photo shoot. The L-shaped sectional sofa is upholstered in Ultrasuede.

Originally built in 1906, the two-story warehouse is located in downtown LA, which itself has undergone a staggering renaissance since 2000. This gentrification includes the conversion of former industrial structures like the Westinghouse building and the Gas Company building into swank residential lofts and most notably the construction of the Frank Gehry–designed Walt Disney Concert Hall, downtown's gleaming newish architectural landmark. The neighborhood wears its charming dichotomy well, reflecting both its historic and architecturally significant past and the newfound vitality of the present. "When we bought eight years ago, we knew we liked the arts district, with its desolate feel," Magnus remembers about the area. "But now we're surrounded by condo lofts and see residents walking their dogs—a most welcome change!"

Before the couple settled on buying the space, they had looked in another LA neighborhood full of history—Hancock Park—but ultimately decided they needed something more mixed use that could also house their wholesale clothing business, Serious Clothing. (Both are self-taught fashion designers who met at a trade show in 1994.) "We thought the plan was simple," laughs Magnus. "We would convert the upstairs to our living space and run Serious downstairs." The now visually arresting colossal loft had great bones but was in severe disrepair after years of neglect. Eighteen months of complete renovation ensued, including sandblasting brick and exposed beams, reglazing skylights and windows, adding all new electrical and plumbing, and refinishing 12,000 square feet of hardwood floors.

**LEFT** Various rooms of the monolithic space whisper modern whimsy and are infused with pop art colors, elements, and furnishings. Most recognizable are Mies van der Rohe's classic Barcelona chairs and daybed (against the far wall). A light fixture made of shells shimmers over a rug fashioned from suede scraps. A vintage chaise upholstered in burnt orange with stainless-steel legs is reminiscent of the perfect 1960s Courrèges dress.

Edgy, slyly hedonistic, and joyfully unpredictable—these words describe the final result: a completely refreshing space that feels genuinely authentic not only to the neighborhood but also to the couple who live there. "The design aesthetic of the loft is our version of a stately English home or a mini Hearst Castle," British-born Magnus appropriately states. Original elements including wood-beamed ceilings and steel casement windows mix with groovy arched doorways, dozens of oriental carpets, and funky hanging light fixtures that emit a charmingly eccentric, tossed-off quality.

Originally the upper level of the loft was two separate buildings—constructed in 1906 and 1925. During renovation, the Walkers cut two openings into the center wall to create better flow between the different sides. A warren of seemingly never-ending rooms with very contradictory personalities now unfolds within. A room full of heavy furnishings rendered in carved wood and velvet upholstery anchors the west end of the home. The east end is offset by areas filled with classic midcentury pieces such as a pair of Mies van der Rohe's Barcelona chairs and Aarnio's hanging acrylic bubble chair. Smack-dab in the middle of the residence is a floating Chinese red boudoir (a guest room), sheathed in white drapes, with a slight air of naughty decadence. This room flows into the kitchen, which serves as a kind of divider between the two sides.

Rather than following one specific aesthetic, the couple was more interested in a "compound-style setup" and in having the design aptly reflect the disparate aspects of their personalities. Huge punches of color from brightly painted walls and several skylights (in the front living room) give the loft the aura of collecting light—a rarity for severe industrial spaces. Striking a theatrical tone without being kitschy, the home's sensibility is all the handiwork of the couple, who opted to forgo using an architect or interior designer. "Karen and I came up with the style and the look," says Magnus. "We've collected things over

**ABOVE** The Walkers' maximalist design scheme is part hookah den, part old-world European cathedral. The elaborately carved bench is from Sweet Smiling Home in LA. The gargoyles, religious artifacts, and flamboyant gold light fixture were found at Architectural Salvage in Harlem.

**OPPOSITE** The couple has created their own version of an urban Hearst Castle, with a gothic-medieval twist: a row of wrought-iron structural braces adds to the illusion. A chair upholstered in heavy green velvet with brass nail detail sits next to a former church pew from the Santa Monica Flea Market.

A decidedly sexy chinoiserie-inspired guest room. The vibe is slightly decadent with imposing paintings by Zoe and a wrought-iron and mustard velvet bench at the foot of the Ikea bed. "Our whole philosophy for decorating was mixing old and new, flea-market finds with designer pieces," says Magnus.

the past ten years from flea markets such as the Rose Bowl and modern furniture suppliers like Modernica and DWR."

And the biggest advantages to having such a megapad? For the Walkers, one favorite benefit might be the opportunity to indulge in another kind of collecting—namely, cars. A portion of the ground floor of the loft is used as a garage to house several sporty vintage Porsches. The garage—and the spectacular home in general—has also spawned an unexpected side business for the couple: over the past few years, they have been renting the loft to television shows (*ER, CSI*), movies (most recently one starring Bruce Willis), and music videos (The Eagles, Van Halen) for filming. "It has proven to be both lucrative and educational," Magnus says, "and very interesting, as the loft is always changed around to look completely different for each project." (The garage has a faux wood laminated floor, designed so that television shows—like *The Contender*, which turned it into a boxing ring—can use the space.)

**ABOVE LEFT** The couple has fashioned a transcendent space, aptly reflecting their passions and creative palette. A mod '70s sofa and matching chairs rendered in white vinyl surround a simple coffee table from Ikea.

**LEFT** In every man's dream, lots of space = lots of cars. Magnus has a place to park his collection of vintage Porsches—which had to be temporarily relocated when the reality television show *The Contender* used the garage as a boxing ring!

**OPPOSITE** Groovy, baby. The couple scoured LA showrooms like Modernica, Room Service, and Futurama for a treasure trove of midcentury design finds, including the black and white leather pod chair and the Sputnik light fixture. The shagadelic round bed was custom made and is outfitted with a red Plexi headboard and fur duvet. The white fiberglass "stand" looks like something straight out of a Dr. Seuss book.

Another enviable urban perk (especially in LA) is Magnus and Karen's rather quick commute time to work . . . about ten seconds down the stairs to their extraordinary office space, also located on the ground floor. "This is great most of the time," offers Magnus, "yet sometimes we find ourselves not having left the building for several days, which can lead to cabin fever!" The couple and their two cats and dog can escape to the private backyard garden, brilliantly reconfigured from a former alley and accessed from the east-end room above.

One can't help but wonder how visitors—the actors, the musicians—respond upon entering this massive and massively creative home. "The reaction we get is normally one of shock," says Magnus, "usually followed by many questions."

**RIGHT** The couple found architectural and structural design inspiration in objects such as the pair of decorative fiberglass carved pieces that flank the arched doorway. This motif also helped set the tone for the rest of the loft. A daybed covered in ornate velvet is wryly suspended by heavy chains. A patchwork of oriental carpets picked up at the Rose Bowl Flea Market casually dots the floor.

As the Rolling Stones famously sing, "You can't always get what you want." Truer words could not be spoken about the notoriously competitive New York real estate market, where buyers are lucky to fulfill even just a few of their home fantasies.

One particularly fortunate couple found their urban dream home a few years ago when they decided to move back to the city from suburbia with their two children—an all the more improbable outcome given the amount of space they were looking for. "My husband and I would take long, long walks at night just going up and down streets looking at buildings and neighborhoods," says the wife when describing their search for the perfect outsized family residence. What they found was an entire floor in one of the most distinguished prewar buildings on Fifth Avenue (originally designed in 1916 by prolific "jazz era" architects Starrett & van Vleck), with unfettered views of Central Park, incredibly running the entire length of the apartment. What they didn't realize, though, was that the real challenge was not the search, but what would follow.

**LEFT** Light bounces off the ebony-colored oak floor in the formal dining room, featuring a custom-made dining table surrounded by Christian Liagre chairs. A Donald Baechler flowerpot sculpture is a whimsical touch placed in front of stunning views of the real thing in Central Park.

**OPPOSITE** The impressive loftlike entrance is unexpected and sexy. The dark round MaxPouf bench by Piet Boon and oversized painting by New York artist Rachel Hovnanian pop off the white backdrop. Exquisite crystal light fixtures were designed by the Dutch company Brand van Egmond.

**LEFT** An "exterior" breakfast kitchen is used for casual family meals; the interior space is fully professional Poliform utilized for large dinners and entertaining. Caesarstone countertops and custom wood cabinetry run throughout.

**ABOVE** Boon designed the sink of stacked white marble and wood rectangular boxes, topped with a copper basin, in the powder room. Paired with an immense wood-framed standing mirror, the objects feel more like a piece of beautiful contemporary art than a place for guests to wash their hands.

**ABOVE** Better than Bergdorf's: Two long rows of white gloss–
painted wardrobe closets were made to measure in the polished
master dressing room. Drawers in the leather-covered bench
conceal the husband's collection of shoes.

**OPPOSITE** A view down the long hallway connecting rooms.
A limestone floor outfitted with made-to-measure woolen rugs
runs beneath exquisitely detailed handmade plaster moldings.

In addition to New York City's torturous building laws,
exclusive co-ops place very strict regulations on renovations.
For this couple it meant adhering to "summer work rules,"
which mandate that heavy construction take place only between
May 21 and September 21. "We have lots of friends who are
designers," the wife says, "but because we wanted to have it
done so quickly, we did not want to hire one of them and then
have it end our friendship." After admiring the work of Piet Boon
in a book, the couple cold-called him. One of the Netherlands'
most high-profile designers, Boon—with his team of architects,
his own furniture workshop and building company—specializes
in carrying out complicated, all-inclusive concepts. (His varied
and complex design projects range from hotels and a limited-
edition Range Rover to a water bottle and a furniture line
available in more than twenty-five countries.) What ensued was
a well-choreographed performance, with up to eighty workmen
and artisans on site every day. The wife and daughter flew to

A rambling, relaxed family room adjacent to the kitchen offers several seating areas, a casual dining table, and an office area. Flexform sofa and armchairs paired with a low-slung B&B Italia coffee table face a made-to-measure fireplace. A floral photo on canvas by Rachel Hovnanian hangs at right.

Amsterdam to stay with Boon and his family. "I learned their aesthetic," she remembers. "By being in their home and visiting other projects they had done . . . to feel their materials . . . it made a big difference, so when their team was not in New York, I could answer the workmen's questions."

Though the previous owners had just completed a renovation, the space had a cold and distant atmosphere, so the new owners gutted the apartment, demolishing and rebuilding all nonstructural walls to restore symmetry to the residence. "The routing was important," says Boon. "We designed spaces that are both intimate and spatial. Large spaces are a challenge, but they are exciting. They allow you to make big gestures." The undeniable balance and the harmonious form are evident immediately, as one stands in the perfectly proportioned entry looking right into the family room/kitchen area or straight ahead into the spectacular length of paired rooms along the park (the dining room and formal living room).

**ABOVE** Boon maximized the excellent light and stellar park views by designing several public rooms along the front of the apartment. The tall white glazed vase is from the Dutch company Mobach, behind which hang custom drapes by Jan Schouten.

**OPPOSITE** Beautifully detailed coffered ceilings were installed by the owners. Beyond the dining room is another sitting room with crisp white slipcovered sofas from B&B Italia. Stark white paintings by Rachel Hovnanian flank the fireplace. Groupings of mirrors hang on either side.

American architect Bill O'Neill and Uberto Construction were also brought in to work on the extensive project. "There were no original moldings left in the apartment, as the previous owners tore everything out—I mean everything," offers the wife. So O'Neill was charged with re-creating and installing exquisitely detailed handmade plaster moldings like those originally conceived for the building. Additional feats of grandeur included hoisting a 2,300-pound bathtub, hand-carved from Italian marble, through a window high above the street.

The final effect perfectly reflects Boon's mantra of "what you see is not design; it's feeling." Rich and international describe the home's formal language . . . a perfect oasis of serenity and peacefulness. Natural light fills the high-ceilinged rooms from all four sides (unheard of for Manhattan). The largely white interior of upholstered furnishings and the limestone tile floors radiate a refined tranquility. Dark ebonized oak floors offer a bit more of a dramatic atmosphere in the dining room. With a warmth and a real human quality, the apartment does feel subtle and effortless at a spectacular six bedrooms, eight bathrooms, and six fireplaces, plus a storage space turned private high-tech gym in the basement.

The enormous amount of space, clean lines, and subdued color scheme also furnish an ideal backdrop for the couple's world-class art collection, which includes works by Donald Baechler, Damien Hirst, and Rachel Hovnanian (the most dramatic of which is surely the starkly beautiful 9-foot photo on canvas of white flowers on black by this New York–based artist). Such luxury surroundings can easily veer into the narcissistic, self-reverential category, but this home instead reflects the authentic understated glamour the popular couple has become known for. It is clear that the heart of the house is the kitchen and adjoining living room. "Most important was a place where we could make a family room/kitchen loft where we could all cook together," says the wife.

As one departs, it is comforting to know that someone has filled such a large home with not only loads of style but also an equal amount of appreciation and joy.

A splash of blue and gray keeps the daughter's room playful and youthful. An eye-catching tall quilted headboard custom made by Piet Boon becomes even more dazzling because of the dreamy Tord Boontje lamp attached to it.

The practice of architecture has always been a highly collaborative one, with the relationship and collective process between architect and client—particularly a residential client—intimate and highly personal. Successful homes, those that genuinely reflect their owners' personalities and passions, are generally born from a close and communicative bond between architect and client.

So, when a Chicago retail investment entrepreneur decided to create a new home in one of the most prestigious old-world high-rises on Lake Shore Drive, he naturally turned to his friend and fellow Art Institute committee member Dirk Denison. Not only is Denison a highly regarded architect and professor at the venerable Illinois Institute of Technology, but he is also an art-world insider, collector, and patron who could appreciate and understand one of his client's chief requests: to design a space to showcase his superlative large-scale contemporary photography collection. (For as Charles Eames famously said, "Design is a plan for arranging elements in such a way as best to accomplish a particular purpose.") "In my work, fine art is very important," says Denison. "Painting, sculpture, ceramics . . . the way that all the design arts are integrated is kind of a template for me. I'm very conscious of an environment where those elements coalesce."

**OPPOSITE** Interior designer Michael Richman layered the apartment with distinctive late deco, midcentury, and contemporary pieces. A cozy, round easy chair covered in white shearling sits below a Picasso. The teal side chair is by Warren McArthur.

Fortunately, Denison had space on his side—almost 8,000 square feet of spectacular lakefront space to be exact—but the apartment had suffered from a somewhat unfortunate significant renovation in the 1970s, when all of the classic original elements (such as moldings and doors) had been removed. Denison's challenge was to somehow restore and pay homage to the vernacular precedent of the 1920s neoclassical jewel. "Layout and proportion in a grand building with good bones are usually very nice," offers Denison. "With this apartment I wanted to bring back the original detail in a chronological way. My architectural elements are there in contrast to the traditional elements of the apartment." Luckily he was able to look at the penthouse unit in the building, which remains in pristine original condition, to assess what was missing and to gather inspiration for his modern reinterpretation.

Significant modifications included lifting all of the door heights, adding detailing elements to match the original design, and restoring wide-plank rift-sawn oak floors (and duplicating them in spaces that were without them). Denison also created more public spaces from what had been six bedrooms and is now three, giving the expansive space a human scale with

**ABOVE LEFT** The chic bar oozes with craftsmanship: Denison used rich figured gumwood throughout and topped the bar with deep Black Beauty stone.

**LEFT** The master closet is a study in sexy minimalist perfection. Exquisite gumwood mixes with slightly transparent etched glass.

**OPPOSITE** The entrance gallery is filled with world-class art and furniture, punctuated by specialized Light Lab recessed lighting. Photos by Thomas Struth face each other on either side of *Coffee Table*, a bronze bench with pewter inlay by Keith Haring. A chair by Richard Artschwager can be seen in the background.

Even the clean and modern kitchen features choice furnishings, such as the Louis Poulsen pendant light. The subtle leather and stainless-steel bar stools are from Ligne Roset, and the center island is covered in Black Beauty stone.

several intimate sitting areas. The idea of circulation and viewing the artwork, much like that of a museum, was also clearly a central focus as many of the transitional spaces have a gallery-esque feeling. "With the help of my curator, Helyn Goldenberg, we were able to display the work exactly how I had envisioned," says the owner. Denison's sleight of hand strikes a sophisticatedly restrained tone—allowing the peaceful view and the captivating art their diva moment. Enormous, often surreal color photographs by important artists such as Andreas Gursky, Thomas Struth, and Rineke Dijkstra stand out next to several twentieth-century master prints and an iconic Dan Flavin fluorescent light sculpture. "I made accommodations for the

collection," Denison says. "I wanted space to flow and be wide open. . . . I also shifted things to have more wall space. It's still a modernist vocabulary, though—very clean and complementary to the art."

The apartment's formal entry leads to a long gallery of art to the right (providing access to the bar and bedrooms on the south side of the floor) and offers entrance to the charming library, high above Lake Shore Drive, to the left. A series of rooms runs along the lake, and following the turn of the drive, the corner office offers 180-degree water vistas. Occupying the central part of the apartment is the kitchen, somewhat separating the public rooms from the more private ones.

**ABOVE LEFT** Photographs by artist Micah Lexier fill the walls of a hallway leading to the guest wing.

**ABOVE RIGHT** The 1920s neoclassical building sits on one of the most coveted sites in Chicago, Lake Shore Drive, with unfettered views of the water and adjacent to Michigan Avenue.

**LEFT** One of Dan Flavin's iconic fluorescent tube sculptures adorns the hallway connecting the public and private rooms of the apartment.

**OPPOSITE** Denison restored the apartment's original library and then raised the door height to accommodate the views of both the lake and the owner's collection of oversized photographs. The gorgeous teak and leather lounge chair is by modernist Danish design legend Hans Wagner and is paired with a chair upholstered in Classic Cloth.

A view through the living room into the office. A custom club series sofa from Brueton in Glant fabric sits behind a Lucid coffee table designed by Michael Richman. Lounge chairs by André Sornay upholstered in Maharam fabric sit on either side. Behind, photographs by Thomas Struth flank the Andreas Gursky hanging in the office.

Materials that exude a distinctly confident masculinity are prevalent, such as the gorgeously crafted gumwood bar and cabinetry and the visually complicated Black Beauty stone used on the bar and kitchen counters, chosen for its figurative and abstract quality. "The bar is my favorite part of the apartment both visually and for its contents," jokes the owner.

Every square foot of the home has been carefully and intelligently crafted. It is obvious that the owner is a serious aesthete, whose appreciation and knowledge extend from photography to the finest furnishings. Chicago designer Michael Richman assisted the owner with the interiors—and the result is one of the most well edited around. "With Michael's leadership, we were able to select wonderful things together," the owner remembers. The readily apparent sensibility bespeaks quality and timelessness. Richman layered in period pieces like a quintessential Donald Judd desk and a Gene Summers dining room table. These extremely special objects create a dialogue of refinement and superior craftsmanship yet are subtle enough to keep from constraining the view or upstaging the art. The space aptly reflects the owner's developed style and his commitment to buying furnishings for their originality and historical significance.

These passions were highlighted by Denison's ability to take his client's interests and create a spectacular architectural backdrop for them. Denison's background and deep appreciation of the fine arts give him the ability to utilize both the scientific and the artistic components at the core of the discipline of architecture. "It was an amazing opportunity to work with someone who allowed the design to combine his outstanding collection with an interplay of modern and traditional vocabularies," says Denison. "For me, the project is simultaneously simple and complex."

**LEFT** In the master bath, the white Thassos marble floor and countertop and the sculptural Boffi bathtub are punctuated only by a pop of color in the Jack Pierson photograph.

The sounds of "Creep" cranking out from a 7,000-square-foot loft in a former hat factory on lower Broadway in Manhattan belong not to Radiohead on an iPod, but to a group of young musicians. Rex and Blu Detiger, ages fourteen and ten, on bass guitar and drums, and Luc, six, on vocals, are paying impressive homage to the rock group in a fantastical futuristic home their friends like to refer to as MTV Cribs.

Jonny and Lisa Detiger wouldn't have it any other way—for themselves or for their hipster brood. Combining intriguing textures like squishy metallic sofas from Ligne Roset with inventive architectural details such as built-in wall pods for the kids to hang out in, the Detigers have created, down to the last detail, a home environment that reflects an expansive, uplifting philosophy. "The vibe Jonny and I wanted is freedom and flow, love and light," says Lisa, who doesn't speak of such things just in the abstract, but seeks their architectural and decorative equivalents. Case in point: original art by Jonny in the living room includes a mirrored orb that blows tuberose-scented bubbles, which the children like to dance under. "We wanted freedom for the kids to express themselves," says Lisa, "and flow for flowing in passion, for watching our children grow, for giving them space to have fun in."

**RIGHT** Originality and idiosyncrasy reign in this home. Jonny's built-in pod seats are the perfect design combination of visually avant garde yet still practical for the young and young at heart. The wall is wood lacquered in black anthracite BMW car paint and hides shelving.

Jonny's silver *Love and Light* bubble sculpture, hanging on the wall at right, blows bubbles of homeopathic remedies—a favorite when the family throws a dance party.

Free-spirited Jonny and Lisa met on a boat in Yugoslavia in 1989, and within months set up house in Amsterdam and later in Ibiza, before moving to New York City, where they lived on Park Avenue for eight years while hunting for the perfect home. "We had Rex just before we decided to move back to New York. Blu and Luc shortly followed," Lisa says. "We were looking for a space that we could gut and redo."

German-born architect Markus Dochantschi, whose studio, MDA, is based in Tribeca, was brought in to supervise the transformation of the loft. Lower Broadway, just blocks from NYU, offered an ideal neighborhood for the Detigers. "We love its culture and character," Lisa says. "It's original, productive, inspiring, and imaginative." When they first encountered it, their future home was sectioned into many rooms, but the walls of this downtown warren soon came tumbling.

Seven thousand square feet is, by U.S. metropolitan area standards, a huge amount to play with, and all those demolished little rooms added up to an enormous space that now gathers ample sunlight. By realizing their unique vision through inventively textured materials and juxtaposing a space-age spareness with luxurious and indulgent furniture and decoration, the Detigers created a fanciful, multilayered world, making each section of the loft count. The family was clever in their use of materials that enabled them to maintain the wide-open loft space but also to visually divide it into different rooms. For instance, separating the kitchen from the living room are strands of metallic beads, and huge white origamilike sheets of a German army fatigue fabric mark the fanciful entry point that is the children's part of the loft. A long hallway leads to each of their bedrooms and culminates in a double-height playroom. The greatest delight and surprise of the children's wing, though, is the secret door (that appears to simply be part of the hallway wall) that opens to reveal a tiny set of AstroTurf-carpeted stairs, which lead to an ingenious guest bedroom overlooking the playroom. (The area is encased in steel and from below appears to be a bedroom befitting George and Judy Jetson.)

**OPPOSITE** The family tends to congregate in the oversized, primarily stainless-steel kitchen to watch their in-residence chef, Jonny, whip up gourmet fare. The stove is by Thermador. The dining room chairs are metal and plywood by Fritz Hansen, and the wood and metal table was custom made by their architect. A simple retractable drape of metal beads creates a transparent curtain separating spaces.

Lisa and Jonny's master suite sits off the main hallway between the kitchen and the kids' wing and contains a bathroom worthy of any swank spa. An über-contemporary gleaming white-tile and stainless-steel powder room is located next to the master suite, and with its double marble sink can accommodate the huge number of guests who tend to descend on the family's popular parties.

Because cavernous spaces, particularly lofts, can feel chilly, the Detigers specifically chose soft, comfortable furniture and colors such as shimmery gold, silver, and cream to warm things up. "We wanted something that was embracing, heavenly and healing to all who enter," says Lisa, smiling. (The result does feel a lot like being wrapped in a warm cocoon.) The glittering, light-hued palette also seems to waken the senses and keeps

all of that good energy circulating. "The colors in our home are very important to us," continues Lisa, who once worked as a textile colorist. "And we wanted our apartment to be very futuristic. Those three colors make you feel better; they're great to live with. Our home is in synch with how we feel."

Architect Dochantschi designed the sink cabinet and supervised the creation of the custom table and chairs in the kitchen and the custom cabinetry in the hallway. A shipping crate containing building materials from Italy, made out of particleboard and stamped HANDLE WITH CARE DETIGERS, has been placed in front of living room sofas, functioning as both a coffee table and a storage chest. Wall pods, ingenious hang-out spaces carved into the hallway alongside spray-lacquered cabinetry, remind Jonny of traditional Dutch sleeping berths. Decorative

**ABOVE** The clean and contemporary monotonal theme carries into the master bath, where silver-accented Kohler marble basins and custom glass tile from Italy glisten. The stainless-steel fixtures are by the storied Danish company Vola.

**RIGHT** The recurring vocabulary of curves and circles adds an air of whimsy and playfulness to the space. The white plastic egg chairs accented with black velvet lining were a gift. Son Rex plays the small teal hand drum handmade in Switzerland.

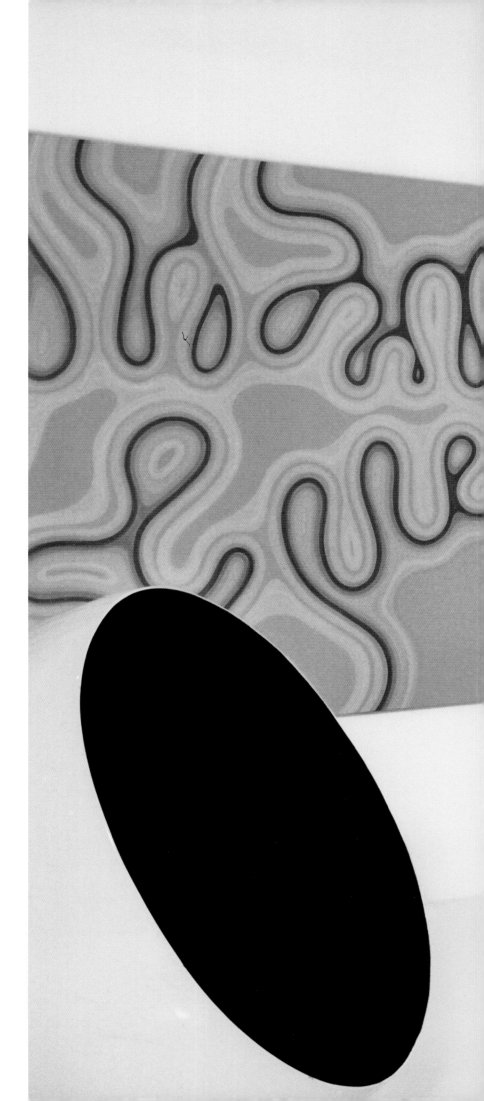

materials and furnishings offer contrast between the soft (Italian Bellora sheets and duvets cover all of the beds) and the slick (white resin floors, marble countertops in the bathroom); between the purely creative (Jonny's biomorphic canvases in the bedrooms, the living room, and the hallway) and the elegantly functional (a blown-glass Venetian pitcher and cups from Murano). All are chosen with an extremely particular eye—flow is more important in this home, says Lisa, than accumulating tchotchkes.

Emphasizing the idea that creativity fuels this family is the front-and-center placement of a Tama drum set and guitars on a white shag carpet in the living room, along with a gilded console table designed by Jonny called Golden Boy (it's got a built-in LP turntable and room to accommodate both a potted fig tree and a Siamese fighting fish). "Our home allows for the playfulness of the child in all of us to be alive," says Lisa. "To live like this with the kids is empowering."

**ABOVE LEFT** Blu, Luc, and Rex Detiger hanging out at home.

**ABOVE RIGHT** Blu's bathroom is, shockingly . . . blue! "The space is all about the kids having freedom to express themselves and to have fun in," describes Lisa. The tub is by Zuma, the sink is by Kohler, and the blue figure is from Kid Robot.

**OPPOSITE** The couple used an unlikely material—white German army fatigue fabric—to create luxurious drapes that separate rooms along the back hallway. The floor is white oak, and one of Jonny's peanut-shaped pod seats created out of lacquered recycled wood can be seen at right. Luc's superhero figures go along for the ride.

The resin floors gleam in the cavernous main entrance hall. Jonny created the built-in pod seats. Several of his paintings lean against the wall at left.

"We did not plan on buying a house of this size!" exclaims the owner of what can only be described as a spectacularly enormous home on one of the poshest streets in San Francisco. "We were not looking to buy at all, but I drove by one day and saw an OPEN HOUSE sign and went in, just out of curiosity. . . . I was fascinated by the elegant bones." The owners, a former model and graduate film student and her real estate developer husband, were living right down the street with their four boys and passed the grand structure almost every day. Originally constructed as a private residence in 1910 by a lumber baron (after the devastating earthquake of 1906), the neoclassical revival building had undergone many contemporary incarnations, most notably as the Russian consulate and as the Delancey Street Foundation—a drug and alcohol rehabilitation clinic. In 2000 it languished on the market, having been broken up inside to accommodate live/work spaces for the nonprofit. "The house was not selling because it was obvious that it was a complete remodel and difficult to envision as a residence," says the German-born wife. "But we saw it as a blank canvas, full of possibility."

**LEFT** Moller Willrich Architects excavated below the original 1910 structure to create a full-size basketball court for the owners' four boys.

**OPPOSITE** The master bedroom features a sitting area with sweeping views of the bay, Angel Island, and the Golden Gate Bridge. Designer Stephen Shubel painted the Venetian plaster walls in saffron, custom fabricating a kidney-shaped sofa in gold velvet to match. The persimmon silk taffeta curtains add a dash of sexy opulence. The cocktail table is vintage 1940s French with a custom leather top and sits on several white cowhide rugs.

Enter Moller Willrich Architecture and Design . . . which actually set up their offices, the year before the renovation began, in what had been Delancey Street's library in order to completely understand the endeavor they were undertaking. "Our office approached the project as both an architectural preservation and a redesign to better serve a family with four young boys and their contemporary lifestyle," Ian Moller says. "Because of the architectural historical classification of the residence, we sought to repair as well as improve upon all of the original neoclassical details," adds Stephen Willrich. To say that this was a complete gut renovation would be a gross understatement. The entire 16,000 square feet, spread over five floors, was utterly rescripted. Every piece of the interior was torn down to the studs. Hand-planed wide-plank walnut floors were installed, exquisite period detailing was restored, and even the sweeping main staircase had to be built from the ground up. Additional challenges included excavating under the house to create an indoor basketball/sports court and cutting back the top floor to fashion an outdoor terrace. One of the few existing original elements that the firm incorporated into their reinterpretation was the masonry fireplaces, which were dismantled for restoration and then reinstalled. Moller Willrich even documented and researched the exterior details, then redesigned them. The home sits on an extraordinary piece of property in San Francisco—a corner lot on one of the highest elevations in Pacific Heights, with breathtaking views—something the architects took full advantage of.

"We were naïve about taking on a project of such scale," remembers the wife. After four grueling years of architect, interior designer, and client working together to revitalize the historical beauty, however, the final product is majestic, with an unpretentious dignity. Most shocking is its transformation into a fresh, inviting, and playful home. The vocabulary is traditional yet light spirited, reflecting the young family. "I was worried that it would feel too formal and serious," the wife offers, "not like us. I wanted our home to be comfortable, bright and welcoming . . . a nest." Of highest priority was a large central and open

The top floor is the most relaxed area in the home, with white denim slipcovered furniture surrounding a metal Indian coffee table.

kitchen, which sits on the second floor and serves as the real nucleus of the home—a place where family and friends can gather, hang out, and be together. This space has an ethereal and airy feeling, awash in white—cabinets, tile, and marble—with a distinctly French country ambience. This level also houses a dining room, a casual dining area and breakfast nook, a living room, a family room, and two powder rooms.

The couple turned to distinguished local designer Stephen Shubel, who had worked with them on their first home fourteen years earlier, to conceptualize a warm and intimate interior within the colossal surroundings. "I found the architecture to be very inspiring," says Shubel. "The sheer size of the residence allowed for a variety of color schemes to coexist; I was inspired by bright intense colors and the client was very open to daring choices of apricots, golds, and oranges." That stunning architecture provided the perfect backdrop for both antiques and new furniture, with a heavily French influence. "Many of the furnishings were found on my travels throughout France," Shubel remembers. "I also searched American antiques sources to find the right pieces."

On the third floor adjacent to the boys' four rooms is the master bedroom. It is lined with handsome bookcases and features robust classical detailing, such as the intricate moldings and an original stone fireplace. Diaphanous tangerine silk drapes and an Indian-inspired bedcover soften things up and strike a bohemian tone. Without a doubt, though, the crown jewel is the laid-back outdoor rooftop terrace—reminiscent of Saint-Tropez's finest beach houses. Simple slipcovered furniture, sun umbrellas, and topiary trees provide a chic surrounding, but the real star of the show is the brilliant view, which commands the entire San Francisco Bay, Golden Gate Bridge, Marin Headlands, and the extraordinary city skyline. And if the notorious Bay Area fog rolls in, the family can retreat into the other rooms on the

**LEFT** The architects created a grand central staircase. Designer Stephen Shubel found the Indian metal console table at the Paris flea market and topped it off with decorative candlestick holders.

Substantial pieces in a bright yet sophisticated palette anchor the living room and suit its grand scale. A custom sofa upholstered in persimmon cotton velvet with hand-carved feet and a custom neoclassical-style daybed with swan carvings flank an ornate Gustavian coffee table with a limestone top. Below sits an antique Oushak carpet. The fireplace mantel is original to the house.

**ABOVE** Shubel chose a delicious blend of fabrics in citrusy hues like orange and lemon that cast the dining room in a joyful burst of light. Elegant custom Louis XV- and XVI-style chairs mix with a more casual, long farmhouse table in hand-planed walnut, also custom made. A pair of French nineteenth-century crystal chandeliers were purchased at a flea market in Paris.

**RIGHT** The master bedroom has an international, bohemian vibe. A custom-made seventeenth-century–style bed is adorned with a silk velvet headboard and Indian-inspired bedcover. An Egyptian-style metal bench sits at the foot. A glorious Fortuny pendant light slightly mirrors the character of the classical moldings and original masonry fireplace.

The second floor features a sunny and bright family room, a sitting room, an additional dining room, and a kitchen. Comfortable armchairs slipcovered in yellow cotton are paired with a woven palm-leaf side table from Ralph Lauren.

top floor: the mostly white lounge room adjoining the terrace—decked out with a full kitchen and a TV area—or the wife's office, the guest suite, and the yoga room.

"I wanted a place to meditate, relax, or retreat with a book," says the wife. With six bedrooms, eleven bathrooms, three dining rooms, a wine cellar, a media room, a full-size indoor basketball court, plus the divine rooftop terrace, she has plenty of options.

But the greatest advantage to this home may actually be the lifestyle it affords in this city with four growing boys. "Luckily San Francisco proper is limited to seven by seven miles, as we drive all over for soccer and lacrosse practices, playdates, and school activities!" says the wife. That, coupled with all of the exciting museums, restaurants, sporting events, and the lush green spaces including Golden Gate Park and the Presidio, makes living here tough to beat. "Living in San Francisco offers both—a city and the outdoors." Having that rooftop terrace doesn't hurt either.

**ABOVE** Moller Willrich wrapped the teak rooftop terrace in glass that protects from the elements but does not impede the outrageous view. Informal deck furniture, topiary trees, and decorative Moroccan fixtures add to the all-out vacation feel.

**OPPOSITE** The kids love to congregate in the family kitchen. The island is made of Statuario marble—a typically white polished stone with veins—and is surrounded by teak stools. Overhead are pendant lights designed by local artisan Jim Misner. The stainless-steel range is from La Cornue.

# THIS BEAUTIFUL DREAM

New York City isn't quite the place that comes to mind when conjuring images of a serene home . . . a Norman Rockwell scene it is not. But somehow Keith and Inga Rubenstein have created a most spectacular urban oasis, a tranquil yet electric abode. Accented by a dazzling collection of contemporary art, the single-family home stands out not only because of the exquisite architectural design, but also because of its grand scale: a total of 8,000 square feet spread out over the home and two outdoor terraces.

"I absolutely love space," says Inga. "It's very peaceful, very calm, this house. I love all the closets! My husband loves the terraces." In this home, the second-floor balcony boasts a grass lawn, and just beyond the master bedroom and bath there's a romantic outdoor shower on a bed of rocks. Says Keith, director of equity investments at Somerset Partners, a private New York–based real estate firm: "We like open spaces, but it's surprising how, with three children, even a large home can sometimes seem small."

**LEFT** Functional yet stylish pieces of modular furniture by iconic designer Jean-Paul Gaultier fill the son's room. An Italian-made sofa, surrounded by drapes made of luxurious wool Donghia fabric, folds out into a bed for sleepovers.

**OPPOSITE** A less inspired architectural design would have left this subterranean room dark and gloomy. The dramatic oxidized-steel skylight cut into the terrace above floats over the living room. The matching pair of silk and velvet sofas with black lacquer frames are from Armani Casa and a custom flower wall inspired by Jeff Koons's work hangs in the rock garden outside.

The view looking back into the home from the small rock garden. The home is a study in structural grace and visual balance, with the various balconies and staircases.

Three years ago, the couple had just finished extensively renovating an apartment in New York City's Battery Park City when Keith discovered that a freestanding home he had admired in a magazine had just landed on the market. Inga had long wished to live in the hustle and bustle of the charming West Village, and got a pleasant surprise while on vacation in Miami. Keith called to tell her that they were moving to their dream home, situated on a quiet street just blocks away from some of the city's trendiest restaurants, such as Da Silvano, and hot boutiques including Marc Jacobs.

Its original structure, a coal truck depot built in the 1900s, had been converted into a commercial garage with two small apartments. In 2003 a real estate executive purchased the building and brought in visionary architect Wayne Turett to turn the entire building into his home. "I was able to transform an old, decrepit space into something contemporary," says Turett, who is known for his attention to detail and use of innovative materials. "My objectives were to bring in as much natural light as possible and to create spacious and tranquil outdoor areas for the client to entertain." To accomplish this, he installed a four-story glass wall in the back. The sturdy glass patio on the second floor doubles as a skylight—the Rubensteins have it tented when they celebrate Inga's Slavic heritage with a blowout bash for Russian New Year, during which the caviar, vodka, and borscht flow nonstop.

**ABOVE LEFT** A visually arresting two-story wood and oxidized-steel bookcase is filled with framed family photos.

**LEFT** Inga and Keith Rubenstein in the master bath.

**OPPOSITE** Turett designed the entire back of the house in grids of glass, which floods the home with sunlight.

**ABOVE** A second-floor sitting room's minimalism is echoed in the plumped stark white leather furnishings from Ligne Roset, offset by a rare collectable Steinway & Sons baby grand piano. A playful painting by Richard Serra is at left; a drawing by Ugo Rondinone hangs on the far wall.

**OPPOSITE** An entrance of bleached maple floors, an open staircase, and unfettered views to the back of the home keep things gloriously light and airy. A hidden door to the right leads into the two-car garage.

A home with this much square footage allocated more vertically than horizontally, and an ample percentage of it outdoors, allowed the architect to make some grand statements, like a dramatic four-story stairway, fashioned out of pine from the original structure, that welcomes visitors as they enter the foyer. Luxurious features include oxidized metalwork done by Gabrielle Shelton at Shelton Studio in Brooklyn, an elevator, all the newest high-tech systems (for security, lighting, air-conditioning, stereos, blinds), an indoor-outdoor koi fish pond, and, in the living room and kitchen, a white man-made stone floor with radiant heat. "I was able to make not just a cosmetic makeover," says Turett, "but to entirely transform the space and realize its potential." Each floor of the home offers something unexpected; for instance, just off the main entrance

is a door leading to a two-car garage, all but unheard of in New York City. The layout of the top floor is equally inconceivable in an urban setting, containing just the master suite, complete with a private terrace off the bathroom.

Since the previous tenant had done most of the architectural refurbishing, all Keith and Inga had to do was decorate. And that they did, with a passion for modern art. It started with just a single Damien Hirst painting that Inga fell in love with at Art Basel Miami Beach, but which was already sold. Keith found a Hirst butterfly piece at Gagosian Gallery a few months later and surprised his wife with it. Suddenly, two serious collectors were born. "Once you catch the art bug, you cannot stop it," says Inga, who joined the international director's council of the Guggenheim Museum in 2007. She and Keith have a stellar collection that includes works by Jeff Koons, John McCracken, Jenny Holzer, Richard Prince, and Salvador Dalí, among other artists—

**ABOVE** The master bedroom, with its Ralph Lauren mink throw and pillows, is straight out of *Doctor Zhivago.*

**RIGHT** "I love the view from the office," declares Inga. The space overlooks both the interior rooms below and the terrace in back, but surely most attention-grabbing is the Sante D'Orazio portrait of a nude, reclining Inga. A Saarinen tulip table by Knoll sits upon a rug made of shredded T-shirts, from ABC Carpet.

plenty to fill the vast wall space. Other great masters of modern art are represented on walls in the living room and the media room (in which a Picasso has a place of honor).

At the heart of the home, on the second story, an office features his-and-hers desks and art by Barbara Kruger—a photograph of candy-colored roses and the words "You Will Never Wake Up From This Beautiful Dream." Says Inga, "When a friend introduced me to Barbara's work, she showed me this and I said, 'I love it so much.' I begged every dealer to get me this piece. And do you know what? Two did, so now I have a pair of them." The other is in storage, but Inga has plenty of wall space, should she decide to double her pleasure. Collecting art and living in a sleek Manhattan megalith is indeed a beautiful dream, she says. "It's my life."

**ABOVE** The winding staircase of oxidized steel and maple creates a graphic maze. Turett added another skylight just above, allowing natural light to filter into each floor.

**OPPOSITE** Part of the original 1800s red brick façade remains intact, giving the home an unassuming yet geographically and historically relevant feel. The stylish maple doors and ivy add a bit of modern panache.

Chicago is often referred to as the Second City, for years trailing New York City in key rankings like population, culture, gastronomy, and sophistication. But in the category of architecture, Chicago continues to hold its own. An architectural force that has helped shape the history of American design, the city features many prominent buildings in a variety of styles, most notably by important architects from Daniel Burnham and Frank Lloyd Wright to Ludwig Mies van der Rohe, Helmut Jahn, and Stanley Tigerman.

In 2000 a new structural masterpiece rose up on the city's lakefront landscape, designed by one of the Midwest's most respected architects, Lucien Lagrange. The eight-story French limestone luxury condominium residence offered a fresh and utterly sophisticated quality of living in an urban setting. Lagrange's classic design embraces a vitality for modern living while incorporating the grace of Chicago's past eras. The building caught the very discerning eye of one of the city's first families—internationally known private investors and their children. "The design was unique for Chicago," says the wife. "We particularly liked the scale and loved the neighborhood on the park."

**LEFT** The formal dining room is one of the many areas in the apartment that provide terrific views of Lake Michigan.

**OPPOSITE** A pair of antique Chinese screens flank a linen upholstered settee in the elevator landing just outside the home's entrance.

**ABOVE** A spacious mirrored private elevator landing leads into the apartment's distinguished formal entry featuring a limestone floor and custom plaster moldings. The six-arm giltwood chandelier is circa 1820 from Austria and hangs over a bespoke hand-carved Cabouca limestone hearth and mantel.

**OPPOSITE** The family can retire to the expansive media room to play pool or watch a movie on the built-in screen (not pictured) while lounging on a sectional sofa upholstered in cream and coffee fabric with rich fur throws.

When the building went up, the couple was expecting another child and needed a fourth bedroom. Having lived downtown for years, they were committed to staying in the city but sought a substantial amount of space to accommodate the family and their many responsibilities. "We required space designed for multiple needs," remembers the wife. "Family areas, entertaining areas, offices, an art studio, a media room, and private bedrooms." They ultimately acquired several units on two levels in the building, combining them for a sprawling houselike upstairs/downstairs effect. That was just a fraction of the custom work the owners would put into their new home: the space was delivered entirely raw, as the developer had intended to allow completely independent and individual build-out by each purchaser. Selecting and collaborating with an architect and interior designer of their own clearly became critical for the family.

Enter David Easton, the distinguished interior designer who began his career working for the iconic furniture designer Edward Wormley and then with the venerable firm of Parish-Hadley, before starting his own firm in 1972. Easton was first hired by the owners in the early '90s, to design a chic hotel and a private club in a popular Colorado ski town. "It has been a wonderful collaboration," Easton offers, when referring to his long-standing relationship with the owners. "But the Chicago project was a challenge—working with an open space completely separate from any previous structure or design idea and giving it the order that it now has." Easton brought in the residential architect Eric J. Smith, with whom he has partnered on various projects over the years, to help undertake the process of creating a logical floor plan and design concept. Complicating matters were issues such as connecting the home to the elevator lobby and to the service elevator and taking full advantage of the unfettered lake views to the east and views over Chicago to the north.

"We worked with David and Eric to create a clear and symmetrical layout, punctuated by circular hallways," says the wife. "The look is traditional in bones and architecture, but pared down, more of a clean and contemporary 'Zen traditional.'" Smith thoughtfully laid out gracious groupings of rooms that create long spaces that divide as one progresses. On the lower level, a private elevator landing leads to the grand formal entry of subtle French limestone floors and exquisite period antiques. Off of this is an entrance to the media suite on one side and down the other, a series of stunning rooms with dramatic views of the lake: an elegant dining room leading into an enormous kitchen, then an intimate family dining room, culminating in the owner's favorite space, a whimsical round sunroom (complete with double-sided fish tank). Long views leading north from this side of the home look through the living room and the library, past a mudroom and a painting studio to a guest suite. Upstairs are the family's private rooms. Easton describes the home as the ultimate space for a twenty-first-century family. "At this point, the ideal space is one big room divided into living and dining, and a library with fireplaces at either end, so you have places for people to sit, watch television, work, and grab a book—all in what is really one large room."

A tranquil color palette and textures used throughout create a peaceful atmosphere that seems to mirror the lake views. Organic materials such as bark paper in the living room, Nordic pine in the library, and wide-plank cerused American white oak floors in the family area provide a nice relaxed contrast to more decorative details including the custom plaster cornice and ceiling ornaments. The wall coverings alternate between refined antique paper, fabric, and simple, beautifully glazed paint. Easton and the owners found specific furnishings all over Europe, the United States, at auction . . . Easton calls it a "big search for a combination of antiques and custom—whatever seemed to fit this part of the twenty-first century!" The home's savvy style—one of taste and culture—is an

**RIGHT** A vaulted-ceiling circular sunroom with infinite lake views has a hint of old-world charm and is easily the most magical room in the apartment. David Easton outfitted the space in relaxed furnishings like a tufted sofa upholstered in herringbone cotton and linen and an assortment of cushioned chairs, surrounding a coffee table by Costello Studio.

A view through the living room culminates in double doors that open to reveal the private library. There is not a trendy furnishing, fitting, or possession in sight—everything is of superlative quality and has a significant meaning or provenance.

**LEFT** The home was designed around a series of long halls. Pictured here is the east hall.

**BELOW** Eric J. Smith's architectural rendering of the lower level helps illustrate how the space flows.

**OPPOSITE** An oversized center island anchors the handsome kitchen. Though built to accommodate a large family that entertains often, it remains cozy and intimate due in large part to the soft periwinkle blue tile that reflects the lake view.

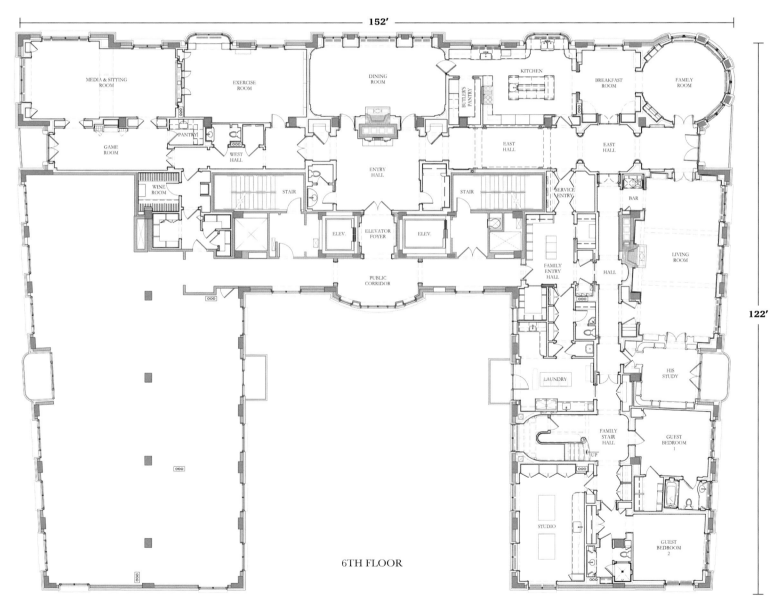

6TH FLOOR

authentic reflection of the distinguished and worldly family who resides within.

Adding to the comfort and convenience is being in a full-service building with a collection of unrivaled amenities: a rooftop landscaped garden of flowers, trees, gazebos, and trellises; heated parking terraces; lovely French windows leading to handmade iron balconies with stellar views of the lake; state-of-the-art prewired technology; and round-the-clock doormen/security. Easton feels that our society is moving toward this type of urban living. "This is an extraordinary trend and one that is logical—as it is difficult to have so many different people working on your home staff and to intelligently manage all services within terms of maintenance," he says. "We have more friends staying in the city with young children and designing great family spaces," adds the wife. "Older friends and empty nesters are also returning to the city." Look out, New York—Chicago may not be second for long.

**OPPOSITE** The formal language of the dining room is custom refinement, featuring timeless pieces such as the fine Louis XVI dining table in mahogany veneer, surrounded by classic cabriolet Louis XVI–style dining chairs in an antique gray shade. Above hangs a nineteenth-century painted wood chandelier, and to the right is a Louis XIV period fireplace mantel made in delicately grained and polished Bourgogne stone. Hand-painted Chinese wallpaper with a bamboo motif covers the walls.

**ABOVE LEFT** A long view down the hallway that runs north, parallel to the living room and library of the home's lower level. Wide-plank cerused white oak floors lend a warm and welcoming air to the substantial space. A brass Georgian-style lantern hangs above.

**LEFT** The smart guest suite is a study in tranquil textures and shades. The bed is dressed in cream Frette linens, a similar shade to the walls upholstered in woven wicker fabric. A leather-topped antique desk sits near the window.

# A FORMER SCHOOL GROWS UP

On a downtown Manhattan block, an anonymous brick façade gives way to one of the most vibrant and stylish spaces to be found on the island of extremes.

Shafts of sunlight filter through a canopy of cherry and lilac trees in the courtyard of the extensive ramble that is artist Izhar Patkin's studio and home. Casually dressed, his eyes sparkling with creative vitality, the artist leans forward in a patio chair and recalls how he came to live in a former Jewish vocational school building, now transformed into a flow of rooms offering a variety of functions and panoramas.

"Seventy years ago, the city sold it to manufacturers," says Patkin, who had been living downtown in another industrial loft, a rental. "When it came up for sale again, a group of us bought the building, then subdivided and renovated it." Guests seeing his nearly 20,000-square-foot home for the first time take a few moments to acclimate to the colorful sanctuary Patkin has created within the urban jungle. "It's a shock for everyone," he admits.

**LEFT** Patkin built the labyrinthlike space around a central courtyard, where a continuous series of rooms lead into each other, most of them with access to the outdoors. The cement floors and wood-beam ceilings are original to the space. On the far wall of this studio are paintings by Patkin from a series called *Madonna Without a Child.*

**OPPOSITE** Almost every room in the home opens out to the garden. "I love being on the ground level—no elevator or stairs," Patkin says. "It makes your relationship to the city more fluid."

Patkin's entrance is decorative and utterly distinctive. The doors, made by a local welder in Chinatown, include sheets of blown glass. To the right are some 200 stools painted in a repetitive pattern that create a mosaic when stacked against the wall. They are not to be mistaken for a work of art, though—the owner simply pulls them out whenever he needs extra chairs.

**ABOVE** Sunlight from the central garden maintains brightness in the cavernous studio, where Patkin's veil paintings hang. The paintings will be shown at a retrospective of the artist's work at the Tel Aviv Museum in 2010. Patkin added the spiral staircase, which leads to the roof garden.

**OPPOSITE** The lower level of the home contains Patkin's art studio, with 20-foot ceilings that enable him to create megalithic works such as this series of paintings on pleated tulle called *Veiled Threats*. Bluestone was recycled from another part of the former school to create the floor. A pair of Eames rocking chairs are at left.

For Patkin, living in an oversized space is a sensible course of action when his creative visions tend toward the monumental. One of his works, *The Black Paintings*, is a room whose four walls are entirely covered in pleated black rubber. (After being shown at the Whitney Biennial in 1987, it is now part of the permanent collection of the Museum of Modern Art.) The Guggenheim owns a life-sized sculpture in anodized aluminum, *Don Quijote Segunda Parte*; another Don Quijote from this series has a place of honor in Patkin's library.

With its multiple studios and gallerylike spaces, as well as an office, the home is perfectly equipped for work, but idyllic pleasures can be enjoyed there too. Says the Israeli-born Patkin: "The biggest dream of growing up in a desert climate is an oasis—this is a bit like that." In one corner of the courtyard, a spiral staircase leads up to a full rooftop garden, where wisteria and grapevines growing on arbors attract the attention of "lots of birds, lots of life . . . cardinals that mate and live here . . . it's a park," Patkin says, adding that he can spend two or

three days at home without ever venturing into the city hubbub.

The task of handling and integrating multiple rooms of varying sizes was clearly no easy feat, especially considering that the circuitous space wraps around a central courtyard—the site of the former school's gym. One has to wonder if the laborious project, especially for a world-class artist, was at all creatively fulfilling. "This house is not art," he says. "Make no mistake. I didn't approach it with the kind of discipline that I'd bring to a painting or a sculpture."

And yet, it's clear that much care has gone into deciding the fate of every surface and corner. In the living room, Patkin's friend painter Kim MacConnell (a key figure in the 1970s pattern and decoration movement) created an oversized green-striped curtain that Patkin likens to both a bamboo forest and a Rothko canvas. Covering the floor here is a burnished carpet created by "an Amish woman who makes rag rugs on a small loom," says Patkin. "I brought her a van load of gold lamé, and asked her to weave rugs from it." The result is exquisitely soft to the touch.

In the kitchen hangs an attention-grabbing chandelier created out of glassware that Patkin had bought as research material for a sculpture. Pitchers, vases, and drinking cups in rich, saturated hues were set upon a series of circular dollies and lit from within. The ingenious chandelier that doubles as a storage space—"a collaged, upside-down dish rack," Patkin says—has inspired imitations by the design world he bypassed in assembling the look of his home.

"This was not about bending the space into a concluded design idea, but seeing the space, looking at what it had to offer," Patkin says. "Until you live in a space, you don't know how it's going to work in your life. I never want to live in a space that's a fait accompli. You grow, you change . . . and so does the space. It's kind of an ongoing weave." Watching an organic process unfold rather than unduly forcing it even affected the

**LEFT** An acrylic on canvas by Kim MacConnell serves as window curtains. Patkin made the two standing chandeliers out of plastic parts.

Ideas and imagination abound in this fantastical home. Above the industrial sink in the kitchen, all eyes are drawn to a chandelier of colored glass cups, vases, ashtrays, and pitchers, which Patkin removes for use daily. At left is a colorful painting by Kim MacConnell of Indian movie stars, and the framed drawing on the right is by Jean-Michel Basquiat.

work of the yearlong renovation crew. None of them proved to be very knowledgeable in tile, so the home contains none.

Past the dining room, a hanging walkway offers a view into a studio where he's working on his current project, a collaboration with the Kashmiri poet Aga Shahid Ali. Huge painted tulle veils of muted black ink scenes inspired by Shahid's poems grace the 20-foot walls. These paintings will appear in Patkin's upcoming career retrospective at the Tel Aviv Museum.

The directness and beauty of the space prompts a visitor to mention that the feeling created is that of a monastery, to which Patkin succinctly replies, "Hardly. There are stories in every room. But they're not meant to hit you over the head with a two-by-four. It's very deep, but lighthearted."

**ABOVE** Bright orange doors to a guest suite reveal stairs that lead to Patkin's double-height studio.

**RIGHT** Sunlight dapples Patkin's rooftop sanctuary, suffused in wisteria and grapevines on arbors, atop the school's former gymnasium.

# PARK AVENUE MEETS THE BOULEVARD SAINT-GERMAIN

When visitors step out of the elevator into Connie and Jeff Tarrant's expansive penthouse duplex apartment, high above the tourist-filled streets of SoHo in New York City, they might expect to see the standard classic loft—tin ceilings, columns, and maybe a little exposed brick. But instead what they find is gloriously unexpected . . . it's as though one has been transported to the surreal intersection between present-day Fifth Avenue and the Boulevard Saint-Germain in 1940s Paris. "I don't like homes where you go in and immediately know the time period it was designed in or the location," says Connie, a German-born fashion illustrator and painter. "If you were to go into my parents' home in Germany, you absolutely could not date it—it is very timeless, and I guess that is what I always try to achieve in my homes." Indeed, the Tarrants' apartment manages to seem traditional yet modern . . . old-world European elegance combines seamlessly with sophisticated contemporary design.

**LEFT** The relaxed upstairs sitting room mixes a bohemian chic vintage Moroccan shag carpet with a baby grand piano and pencil and ink on paper.

**OPPOSITE** Paneled double doors open from the living room, providing long views through the apartment, more reminiscent of a prewar European home than a modern New York City loft. The marble-tiled entry is gracious yet informal.

Connie and her husband, Jeff, an investor, found the generous and very raw space (complete with concrete floors) in 1998 after deciding that they needed a formal family home when their second daughter was a baby (Paulina is now fifteen and Fabienne is twelve). When they began designing, many of Connie's friends did not understand why she wanted to break up the space and create rooms, but she says, "At this point in our lives we need privacy and a real family home, with large doors and thick, solid walls. And the duplex works perfectly for us—the entertainment space and bedrooms are far apart, and I can also be in the back in my office and not feel that there is even help in the house. And most important, the children have space to play and run."

But starting with a totally blank canvas and creating a harmonious space that mixes downtown hip with uptown chic was a

**ABOVE** In the peaceful cream master bedroom, antique mirrored doors with custom hardware conceal Jeff's home office. French doors to the left lead to one of the apartment's four terraces. The quilted headboard was custom-designed by Aero.

**OPPOSITE** To keep things fresh, the Tarrants and their designer, Thomas O'Brien, opted for a pair of small console tables from Coconut and Company, instead of a more predictable formal dining room table, keeping the open, airy space chic and simple. A set of curvy chairs custom made by Aero and modeled after a vintage pair provides the perfect complement.

tall order. Finding the perfect architect and designer was essential. "I had heard about Thomas O'Brien and his firm, Aero, when I first moved to New York," remembers Connie. "Then I fell in love with his shop on Spring Street . . . his colors, his style. When we decided to build the apartment, I just knew that it had to be him!" O'Brien has become the designer of choice for many well-heeled New Yorkers, fashioning residences for bold-faced names such as Giorgio Armani (his oft-published Central Park West aerie), and has branched out into restaurants and hotels, such as 60 Thompson. A trip through his décor-filled shop confirms his standing as an arbiter of good taste and fine living.

The design concept for the entire apartment started, surprisingly, with the oversized floating island in the kitchen. "I saw this very piece that Thomas had designed in his shop and thought it was perfect for the kitchen—which I wanted to be the real heart of the apartment, with lots of space to hang out," Connie says. That piece, made of walnut and steel on wheels, and the vast and utterly charming kitchen in general, ended up representing a kind of design theme for the Tarrants: comfortable, cozy, and private. "The girls sit in here to do their homework, this is where we have casual family dinners, and friends come by and don't want to leave the kitchen!" The room oozes O'Brien's trademark classic warm modernism and immediately puts a smile on visitors' faces.

"Connie just has this great eye," says O'Brien. "She's a savvy, stylish person, and I was constantly amazed at the things that she would find. And the space is so magical—four terraces off of both sides of the apartment! Never do you see that. It's really a house in the sky." O'Brien also did not shrink from Connie's love of combining furnishings with divergent genres and styles.

**RIGHT** Connie wanted the outsized kitchen to be the "heart of the apartment." Aero used the vast walnut and stainless-steel floating island as design inspiration for the rest of the home. Next to the double Viking range are convenient refrigerated drawers. Overhead hangs an urban-looking 1930s pendant light fixture.

"Most of our clients like to mix things up now," O'Brien offers, "but it's all about balance. With the Tarrants' apartment, we blended all of those ideas and made it personal for them . . . those are elements that are important to them and are things I like, too."

O'Brien's words aptly describe the blue living room, which has a very personal origin. Just before starting work on their new home, the couple saw an old Ingrid Bergman film that included a Parisian apartment with blue walls, and immediately knew that they wanted to incorporate the color somehow. The hue creates a serene sitting and entertaining area, and soft light filters through diaphanous cream drapes that conceal the largest terrace, with views of the Empire State Building. Small

**ABOVE** Light floods the elegant living room, bedecked with an upholstered sofa designed by Thomas O'Brien. Connie found a velvet-lined antique display case that she turned into a coffee table filled with shells. A Balinese daybed on the terrace (visible through the windows) offers a magnificent spot for lounging.

**OPPOSITE** Gauzy silk drapes grace the long hallway leading to the master bedroom, transcending a specific time period or genre. A pair of sumptuous upholstered benches was fabricated by Aero.

touches, like the vintage display case/cocktail table filled with starfish and seashells, keep the space fresh. "We really wanted to keep that young feeling," says O'Brien.

It is also readily apparent that he gave considerable thought to how one room flows into the next and to the views from room to room throughout the space. (O'Brien left the layout open enough for sight lines to run all the way from the front terrace to the back terrace.) The generous proportions, extra-high ceilings, and clean lines are reminiscent of a grand Emery Roth building on Central Park West, though not very many Roth apartments boast this much breathing room.

Upstairs are the bedrooms, including Fabienne's, with her custom-made two-story bed—part tree house, part playroom— and a jaw-dropping glass atrium fabricated in England, which served as Connie's painting studio. Just off the atrium, a groovy guest room is outfitted with a vintage Moroccan shag carpet, a baby grand piano, and a magnificent pair of black-lacquered Dorothy Draper consoles. The real surprise upstairs, though, is Jeff's hidden home office within the master bedroom suite. The secret location, multiple computer screens, and leather walls give the private oasis a masculine feel befitting 007.

**ABOVE LEFT** Family photos adorn Jeff's handsome leather-paneled home office oasis.

**LEFT** "Four terraces off both sides of the apartment! Never do you see that," exclaims designer Thomas O'Brien. The largest of the four terraces faces northwest, with stellar skyline views of the Empire State Building and New York's iconic water towers.

**OPPOSITE** An elegant chandelier is offset by the playful bunk bed-cum-tree house in daughter Fabienne's girly bedroom.

Secreting away all the mechanics for an apartment of this size proved more challenging, however. The couple decided to split up equipment like the air-conditioning units, concealing a portion in the ceiling of the nanny's room, some in a tiny room near the front door, and the rest on the roof. . . . Other items they simply decided to do without. "I remember that we had a problem placing the central vacuum—and that's why we just don't have one!" exclaims Connie.

When asked her favorite thing about having so much room, Connie replies, "I love my outdoor space—that I can have an herb garden next to my kitchen, lots of flowers, and blue sky when I step outside." In fact, the Tarrants seem to be part of the group reversing the trend of having kids and leaving the city confines for the suburbs. "Many of my friends have purchased very large apartments and townhouses to be able to stay in the city with their families. Very few people I know move out to the country now." With four terraces, what would be the point?

**ABOVE** Light floods the expansive kitchen from a wall of windows on either side of the table.

**LEFT** Hidden on the second floor is a glass conservatory fabricated by Hope's Windows in Jamestown, New York, where Connie painted until 9/11. (She now has a studio in Tribeca.) Both the atrium and the adjoining terrace have unfettered Manhattan skyline views west, south—where the World Trade Center once stood—and east.

When a high-tech wizard decides to leave his rambling home high in the hills above Silicon Valley and move back to the metropolis of Miami, one word comes to mind: *downsize*. Luckily, not for Alex Daly. "My home in the Saratoga Hills was about six thousand square feet on three levels, with spectacular views," explains Daly. 'After you become used to living in a large home, I think it's difficult to go back to something less spacious." So Daly went out and found himself an even *larger* abode . . . located on the water and thirty-five stories up in the sky, no less.

Built in 1997, Daly's newfound home—the Santa Maria—caused quite a stir when it opened. The building was considered legendary developer Hugo Columbo's labor of love . . . a high-rise of luxury and amenities never before seen in the U.S. With a nod to both the property's rich past as well as its exciting future, Columbo built on the same dramatic waterfront property where longtime Miami mayor Maurice Ferre's beautiful Mediterranean-style villa sits— maintaining the architecturally and historically significant home in its original form. (Residents now use it for private events.) The world-class views from the condominium include an expanse of water on one side, downtown Miami on the other. Known for its high level of security and privacy, the building is home to many celebrities. As Daly says, "I travel often and it's great to know that I can just drop off my keys and go without any worries."

**OPPOSITE** A fluid and floating metal light fixture by David Weeks is the perfect complement to the double-height ceiling, but without obstructing the flawless Biscayne Bay views.

Daly's apartment boasts expansive water views from the double-height living room. His interior designer custom made the textured white nubby raw-silk sofa and matching chairs. A Cascata coffee table fabricated from hundred-year-old seasoned Italian walnut sits on a metal-colored Stark shag carpet.

Though born in New York City, Daly is a Miami boy at heart, having grown up there and attended the University of Miami. After spending fifteen years making his mark in the digital world in California, he decided to return to this Florida city in 2000 to be closer to his family. He remembers, though, immediately wondering how he could maintain the lifestyle he had become accustomed to out west: square footage wasn't really the ultimate goal; it was a feeling of openness and killer views. And he had one other tiny request—a slip for his Pershing yacht, *Razzo*. "I am very spontaneous, so if I had to drive to a yacht club, I would probably use the boat much less frequently," Daly explains. "Some days I just look out my window and see that it's a perfect day for boating. . . . I simply take the elevator and in five minutes I am on *Razzo*." Full service, indeed.

Daly's striking thirty-fifth-floor duplex aerie boasts multiple balconies on both levels that survey 270 degrees of water and Miami skyline . . . "so you can follow the sun if you so choose," he says. The double-height glass windows follow the curve of the building, adding to the illusion of space, creating interesting angles in the unit. Daly brought in prominent designer Sam Robin, best known for glamorous high-profile projects such as the Versace boutiques worldwide and private jet design for international bon vivants Sheik Mohammed of Dubai and Adnan Kashoggi. "It's not about having a certain number of rooms,"

**ABOVE LEFT** Club chairs upholstered in buttery Spinneybeck leather are gathered around a circular walnut cocktail table in the library.

**ABOVE RIGHT** On the lower level, an art-filled hallway connects the living room and dining area. A painting by Belgian artist Rudi Pillen hangs above a hundred-year-old Italian walnut console, flanked by mid-eighteenth-century Chinese emperor chairs.

**OPPOSITE** Elements like the high ceilings, immense windows, and a floating glass staircase are anchored by the dark rift-cut oak and Wenge wall paneling. The stainless-steel staircase rail was custom made by designers of yacht fixtures. An interior window from Daly's office looks down over the living room.

The masculine custom millwork done by artisans from Colombia provides perfect balance to the flood of sunlight in the dining room. Designer Sam Robin paired a Sienna antique chestnut dining table, custom made by her firm, Sirio, with casual woven wicker chairs softened up with chic white linen cushions. Daly's own photos from Cuba dot the far wall, and masks that he found in Venice are displayed on the table.

The commanding visual focal point in the opulent yet masculine office is Daly's sleek multihued German-made wood desk, modeled after a similar 1950s piece. Colombian artist Marcia Conzo's provocative nude painting sexes up the room.

**ABOVE** Built in 1997, the architecturally innovative and über-exclusive Santa Maria boasts some of the largest residences in South Florida and sits on a dramatic and pricey piece of water-front property.

**OPPOSITE** One of the Santa Maria's biggest perks is parking for Daly's yacht at the building's private dock.

Robin modestly offers with regard to the apartment. "It's about the feeling of being open to the elements of water . . . the sky . . . the view . . . whatever blends the inside with the outside." (Daly does admit that "the openness frees my mind to think and create more effectively.") Using natural materials and aged woods, Robin embued the interior with a sense of timelessness. It is sophisticated yet simple, striking that difficult-to-achieve marriage of feminine and masculine. Immense sunlight and elements such as high ceilings and a floating glass staircase are anchored by the darkness of rift-cut oak and Wenge wall paneling, created by artisans from Colombia. Many of the more powerful pieces were custom made by Robin's company, Sirio; these include the Italian walnut tables fabricated in Perugia, Italy, and the distinctly rich desk in Daly's office, made by a master craftsman in Germany. The color palette (lots of cream, beige, and sable brown) and texture scheme are neutral, but Daly's eclectic art and graphic accoutrements add a dash of the theatrical, most evident in the fluid metal David Weeks chandelier–cum–light fixture hanging in the two-story living room.

"Working with Sam was great in that she fulfilled the vision for how I wanted each room to 'feel,'" says Daly. Every nuance was discussed, down to the stainless-steel staircase rail custom made by designers of yacht fixtures. Possibly owing to his status as a popular bachelor-about-town, Daly wanted a sensuous and warm master bedroom, so Robin paired soft suede walls—usually a modern motif—with earth-toned fabrics for a stylish yet inviting result.

Perfectly proportioned rooms lend the space an overall poise, making it apparent that no area of the apartment was an afterthought (an all too common casualty in large homes). Daly and Robin succeeded in dividing the spaces into distinct areas, featuring a variety of moods. "It's fun to entertain here, as guests tend to migrate to their own particular favorite areas," he

explains. "The library and living room are great for conversation. The dining room is a wide space with great views of the city— and its 'carpet of lights' at night. The balconies are peaceful and inspirational." And Daly's preferred place to kick back? The media room, of course (see bachelor reference above), decked out with the requisite high-definition screen and high-fidelity sound system. "It's the perfect place to wind down at the end of the day, catch a movie, or just listen to music," he says.

One can't help but wonder if all those different moods of all those different rooms, spread out over a whopping amount of square feet, ever feel like too much space for one guy. The home begs that age-old question: Is bigger indeed always better? "Not necessarily," Daly reflects. "Like all things, whether large or small, what matters is the coherence of the space, its livability and the feelings that it creates within you."

# A LUSH NOD TO COUNTRY LIFE

A discerning individual might look at an old, grand, and gorgeous warehouse that once housed a shoe importer and wholesaler and think "home." Few would have the means to transform a utilitarian shell into an upscale apartment building with a luxe triplex penthouse. And a tiny percentage among them would have the chutzpah to literally raise the roof—on a landmark building in the posh Tribeca section of Manhattan, no less—and make an already sumptuous living space even more spectacular, complete with a thriving garden.

But then, Stephen Corelli is far from ordinary. Born and raised in Canada, educated at the University of Toronto, the Architectural Association in London, and Princeton University (where he received his graduate degree), Stephen worked for the likes of Michael Graves, Eisenman/Robertson Architects, and the Polshek Partnership Architects before opening his own practice, with partner Michaela Deiss, in 1987. He's a strategic visionary, part detective, part creator, part translator. "Having designed more than a hundred apartments in the last twenty years," he says, "I have worked on a range of different scales and budgets, but am always trying to find the most compelling narrative for each home, regardless of its size."

**OPPOSITE** A mezzanine billiards parlor sits above the professional-grade Bulthaup kitchen. Corelli can enjoy a casual dinner on one of the stools designed by Shin Azumi, fashioned from stainless-steel LEM piston rods and leather.

For his own residence, he decided to go huge—adding two stories to the top of what was originally a five-story building that he first laid eyes upon in 1999. "The forty-two-foot-wide building—an unusual size, when many lofts of this type are twenty feet in width—was constructed in 1859," he says. "My office is a short distance from the property, so I decided to acquire, renovate, and convert the building to apartments, retaining the upper floors for myself."

The generous heft of the building, by New York standards, at 100 feet deep, necessitated special planning for proper circulation of light and air because windows existed only on the front and back. Stephen's strategy was to create rental apartments on the second, third, and fourth floors, with a public stairway and elevator dividing the spaces. His own living quarters are located on the fifth and newly added sixth and seventh floors, totaling 8,000 square feet of interior space. Removing the roof not only gave him precious extra square footage but also allowed him to reconfigure the size and layout of the rooms, resulting in the creation of a living room with 30-foot, three-story-high ceilings. This "apartment surgery" offered some surprising aesthetic benefits. Stones uncovered

**ABOVE LEFT** The majestic limestone structure dates to 1859. Corelli lifted off the roof—adding two stories to the top—to create the now 8,000-square-foot penthouse.

**LEFT** A set of 1940s cherry red leather chairs stands out against the geometric patterns of the stairs and the heat-blackened, hand-rubbed steel railings.

**OPPOSITE** Corelli reimagined the classic pool hall; his version is polished and elegant for an aesthete billiards aficionado. His architecture firm, Triarch, designed the pool table and had it manufactured by Blatt Billiards. A pair of sublime light fixtures from Dutruc-Rosset in Paris hang over the table.

A view of the lower level of the apartment from the mezzanine.
LA designer Kerry Joyce created the elegant armoire against the wall.
Photos from Ken Wong's *Yosemite Series* hang on either side.

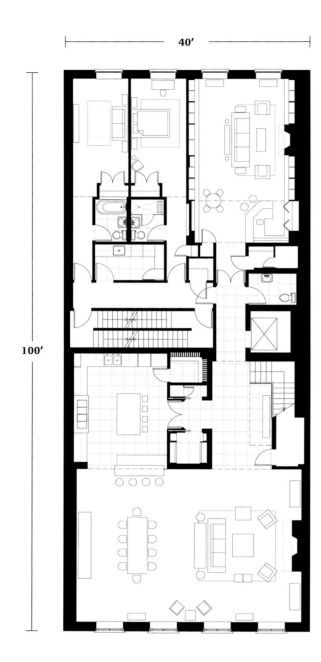

**ABOVE** The first-floor architectural renderings help convey the layout of the enormous 40 x 100-foot space.

**RIGHT** Corelli was able to utilize stone from the original wall of the building in his renovation, maintaining authenticity and grace. He chose design elements with a distinct French deco character, like the quarter-sawn, limned oak paneling and the portero marble fireplace. The antique Tabriz carpet was bought at Sotheby's, and the pale ocher upholstered sofa and matching chairs were designed by Kerry Joyce. A row of skylights makes use of the penthouse perch, affording copious sunlight.

**ABOVE** A secluded office sits off the master bedroom. Corelli purchased the distinctive white bed footboard, based on a Jean Michel Frank design, at a Christie's auction. Voluminous custom-made brushed-silk drapes pull back to reveal the terrace.

**OPPOSITE** The old-world masculine glamour of the library is expressed in the quilted leather–covered doors and handsome wood paneling.

at the back cornice of the building were revealed to be raw and uncarved. Moved to the front of the building, "they animated the space," Stephen says.

A variance helped him surmount most of the red tape attached to working with a landmark building, specifically a Civil War–era loft. He was able to build his addition, but with the proviso that it be set back 12 feet from the street wall. "That requirement resulted in the creation of a thirty-by-twenty-foot volume in which the primary living space is contained," Stephen explains. Above the addition perches a gray stucco structure with its own kitchen next to a garden containing three cherry trees and wisteria that thrives in the spring and summer.

Even with this lush nod to country life, Stephen sees his home as urban in construction and character. "Most significantly, the space is created from the raw material of an obsolete loft building. Certain elements of the existing structure, such as the stone wall and steel trusses in the living room, refer back to the original character of the building," he says. "These elements contrast with some of the other materials, which are highly refined and carefully detailed." Choosing all the decorative elements himself, Stephen referenced 1930s and '40 s Manhattan style, filling the space with luxurious details like quarter-sawn limned oak paneling in the living room and Wenge flooring. "I'm responsible, or to blame, depending on who you talk to," he jokes. In the entrance foyer, kitchen, and powder room, French limestone has been polished to a high gloss. Symmetry rules in a delineation of space that is highly graphic and soothing, with wooden and golden tones layered with whites and creams. Rooms are allowed to sprawl, as on the first floor, which flows between living room, dining room, and a state-of-the-art Food Network–worthy kitchen. ("I cook mostly for friends . . . there are a lot of great restaurants in the neighborhood," Stephen says.) Ample space is given over to pursuits of leisure, study, and play—a makore-paneled, sisal-carpeted library; a game room with a pool table fashioned out of quarter-sawn limned oak paneling, also found on the stairwell.

"The layout recalls some of the strategies employed by architects responsible for the better prewar buildings developed in Manhattan," Stephen notes, citing James Carpenter and Mott Schmidt as influences. "Having a large amount of space in a city as congested and vibrant as New York is certainly in and of itself a great luxury, but what I find most compelling about the apartment is the way movement through the space unfolds to create a kind of promenade."

**RIGHT** Because landmark laws stipulated that Corelli have his top-floor addition set back, he created an urban rooftop sanctuary for relaxing and grilling. The apartment also has a terrace off the master bedroom on the south side of the building.

"I travel so much I just got used to hotel living!" exclaims Loree Rodkin, describing the catalyst behind her recent move from freestanding home to sprawling high-rise in Los Angeles. "I quite like the idea of a full-service, security-oriented building like the iconic Sierra Towers. And it was all about the luxury of space, really." Girl-about-town and well-known jeweler to the stars Rodkin had been living in a spectacular yet minimal home tucked away high in the Hollywood Hills, complete with fabulous yard and pool. But in 2007 Rodkin decided to change her lifestyle, buying in arguably the best-known and most celeb-studded building right off of LA's notorious Sunset Strip.

The Modernist landmarked Sierra Towers was built in 1965 and has become a status symbol for the chic set—the same select group you might find down the street at the sophisticated yet low-key Tower Bar. (Two of Rodkin's close friends—Sir Elton John and Cher—have reportedly purchased apartments in the building recently.) At thirty-two stories, the singular apartment building is set back at the intersection of Doheny and Sunset, at the foot of the

**LEFT** The Modernist landmarked Sierra Towers rises high above the intersection of Doheny and Sunset—at the foot of the hill from which Beverly Hills originally derived its name.

**OPPOSITE** Rodkin selected soft and sumptuous upholstery and fabrics that warm up the honed limestone floors. A Holly Hunt chenille sofa rests on a white goat rug. The built-in Macassar ebony bookcase houses a collection of Balinese pots and petrified wood wheels found in Borneo.

**LEFT** The dining room and terrace feature limitless views of Beverly Hills and Century City.

**ABOVE** A view down the grass-cloth–covered hallway culminates in a decorative wood carving found in Bali.

**ABOVE** Rodkin's aesthetic is a sophisticated mix of Balinese elements and muted textural fabrics. "I don't like chaos in my house," says Rodkin. "Serenity is more important to me." In the living room the Holly Hunt sofa in woven chenille is paired with an oak coffee table designed by Martyn Lawrence Bullard. Tree branches in a teak vase from Andrianna Home in New York City sit next to an antique Balinese drum from Primary Source in LA.

**OPPOSITE** Rodkin's "Zen modernist" home is all about tranquility but with urban tribal overtones. The rich Wenge dining room table is from Armani Casa, over which hang basket lights from Rewire in LA. Photos on canvas by Brian English of the Herb Ritts Foundation line the kitchen.

hill from which Beverly Hills originally derived its name. The stucco and glass structure is fifteen stories taller than any building in a two-mile radius and one of the tallest in greater Los Angeles (based on altitude relative to sea level), providing unparalleled views spanning all the way from downtown to the ocean. But those views will cost you . . . at $2,000 a square foot, the Sierra Towers contains some of the priciest real estate in all of Southern California.

Rodkin first bought one apartment but immediately realized she needed more space. "I tortured my broker into stalking the people who owned the apartment next door—it wasn't for sale—but I think they sold to me so I would leave them alone . . . that, and I made them an offer they couldn't refuse." She combined the two rambling units—gutting everything down to the frame. The result is the epitome of contemporary city living

The distinct shapes, hues, and designs in the materials Rodkin chose work together in a cohesive manner. The grass-cloth wall coverings playfully mix with the contradictory design of the Macassar ebony walls, opposite. A Brian English photo on canvas hangs at left.

in LA; if you had a Spanish-style home in the '90s and went midcentury modern in 2000, an expansive full-service home in the sky seems to be the next step for current design aesthetes.

The 7,000-square-foot space is vast but broken into intimate living areas, which allows it to feel open yet maintains privacy at the same time. The gracious, loftlike layout was clearly well planned, as it provides long views from room to room—in some cases the entire length of the apartment—often culminating in floor-to-ceiling windows and drop-dead views of the LA skyline. The dining room boasts seamless corner windows with a jaw-dropping 180-degree vista of Hollywood, Beverly Hills, and Century City. A 2,000-square-foot terrace wraps around several sides of the unit, providing views east, west, and south.

LA is all about the illusion of fantasy, and Rodkin has created an environment that aptly reflects her hometown: it's an ethereal and dreamy space where a visitor feels transported to some far-off land—maybe a Thai princess's twenty-first-century urban castle. The recurring design vocabulary is Asian-inspired serenity. "I'm a Zen-modernist," says Rodkin. "I wanted the peace and tranquility of my former Balinese house, but with a sophisticated modern palette. I describe my apartment as being a study in the absence of color, with a tribal modern twist. Cher always refers to my color palette as mouse-colored, and she's spot on. We call it 'the house of the mouse.'"

These are couture surroundings, to be sure. Rich materials abound, as in the Macassar ebony bookcases in the living room, grass-cloth wall coverings, and exotic custom Lagos Azul limestone flooring throughout. Rodkin, who in a former life was an interior designer for the likes of Rod Stewart and Alice Cooper, is of that rare breed able to help design the home and furnishings as well as manage the project. In fact, her great strength may be the fact that she is not a classically trained interior designer or architect: for her, anything is possible and she doesn't seem limited by what a professional might think is

**RIGHT** Rodkin's custom Poliform closet houses her extensive collection of clothing.

right or wrong. For this new apartment, Rodkin came up with her own personalized, innovative concept—an ever more important thing in the design world—and had the courage to take some chances. "I was my own architect," Rodkin offers. "As for interior design, I brought my friend Martyn Lawrence Bullard on board to be my second set of eyes and to manufacture my soft furnishings. I always design my own furniture because I'm very specific . . . a little princess and the pea—sofa's too hard, not deep enough . . . I can drive a workshop mad."

She mixes lots of textural woven fabrics, custom-made chenilles, suede, and rare skins including elephant hide, sheared rabbit, and goatskin rugs. Hidden in the far reaches of the apartment, the master bedroom serves as a peaceful retreat from the constant motion of Rodkin's demanding design career (which now includes eyewear, fragrances, high-end handbags, and the Beverly Hills hotspot Luau) and social calendar. But the pièce de résistance in her residence must be the master closet, which boasts more square footage, seating, and art than many boutiques on Rodeo Drive. "I needed a closet the size of most people's homes," laughs Rodkin, "to house my fashion addiction—my retail obsession."

Loree Land is outré, constantly violating convention, and that's what makes it spectacular, intriguing, and most definitely different. How often does one see a home in which the master closet is larger than the living room?

**ABOVE LEFT** Loree Rodkin at home in her Sierra Towers apartment.

**LEFT** In the master bedroom, Rodkin created the headboard using suede from Edelman. The funky oversized bedside lamps are made out of coconut and were found in Bali.

**OPPOSITE** "I love the luxury of a huge bathroom," Rodkin offers. "I like it to be something that you can lounge in." Her signature for adding a dash of the unexpected can be found in the fur rug and the cabinet pulls made from Balinese shells set into bronze.

# MEATPACKING MODERN

A single sheet of weathered rolled Cor-Ten steel weighing 17 tons covers the façade of a landmark building in Manhattan's Meatpacking District. Gritty, idiosyncratic, and utilitarian, 40 by 14 feet and 1½ inches thick, the steel slab functions not only as ornamentation but also as a privacy protector. It's a cool camouflage, a grand statement for a five-bedroom, four-and-a-half-bath townhouse.

Five stories tall, this residence is a rarity in New York—a home rebuilt from the ground up. On the original site stood a Federal-style townhouse, 20 feet by 60 feet, constructed in 1856. The home, which had once been connected to a coal and firewood yard, lost most of its original detail when it was converted to a loft building. Last occupied in 1985, it had fallen into a state of extreme disrepair.

**LEFT** Baird found and preserved the original stone foundation walls of the 1856 house (visible at right). A tiny balcony on the ground floor looks down on the spectacular basement media room with 21-foot ceilings.

**OPPOSITE** Arguably the home's most distinctive design element is the façade. A single piece of recycled steel plate runs up the front. To transport the plate into the city, several lanes of the George Washington Bridge needed to be shut down.

Leading to the back garden, an oversized wall of windows (which completely retracts accordion-style) gives the home an open yet private feeling. The polished stainless-steel Boffi and Sub-Zero kitchen adds a punch of panache coupled with the more raw cast-in-place concrete island.

**ABOVE** "Creating a house of 6,000 square feet, with 5 bedrooms and 4.5 baths, and have it still feel open was a design challenge," admits Baird. He installed massive sliding East Indian laurel wood doors that give the house an open loftlike feel when drawn back. Light streams in the solid glass rear of the home.

**OPPOSITE** Baird created long vertical views within the home, using double-height spaces where possible. Industrial-looking concrete stairs were covered with a woven leather runner, typically used as a drive belt in textile mills. The wood door at right slides back to reveal the garage.

The new owners, a European couple with three small children, first saw the building with a "for sale" sign when exiting the hip French bistro Pastis across the street one night. Twenty-four hours later they bid on the property, buying it for $1.6 million, and before they could even begin construction, the building's shell came crashing down on its own and the city was called in to demolish the remains.

Envisioning a sophisticated, modern home—not necessarily the easiest aesthetic to get past the notoriously tough Greenwich Village Society for Historic Preservation—the couple met with more than twenty architects until they found Matt Baird, whose most recent project at the time (with Tod Williams, Billie Tsien & Associates) was another ground-up renovation, the much-celebrated American Museum of Folk Art in New York. This 40-foot-wide, 6-story, 12,500-square-foot gallery space was completed in 2001 to resounding acclaim (winning citations such as *World Architecture* magazine's Best Building in the World, 2002, and one of *Time* magazine's Top Ten buildings of 2002). Baird, who had studied architecture at Princeton and Columbia, was recommended to the couple by a friend.

His plan for the property, he says, was based upon the idea of an airy structure that would be both open and private, a mandate that led to the street façade of recycled steel. (Installed in a single morning, the slab was so heavy and unwieldy that inbound lanes on one level of the George Washington Bridge were closed in order to haul it in.) The back of the home would serve as the primary light collector; all glass, its panes of varying shapes fit together like a transparent Mondrian. Half of the home's roof is a giant skylight, which pours light down to even the lowest levels of the house.

The central design theme of allowing light into the home yet keeping it private is continued with two floor-to-ceiling lot-line windows, providing diagonal views up and down the street while obscuring direct sight into the house. A series of meditative landscape photographs by Olafur Eliasson adorn the far wall.

Baird did face a formidable design challenge, though: how to craft an expansive-feeling five-bedroom home of more than 6,000 square feet out of a 20-by-60-foot dense city lot. It took seven months to plan and eighteen months to build. "We pursued a couple of different approaches to get all that extra square footage," Baird says. "We dug down to create a basement floor with the great room, capturing additional space. We also created long vertical views with windows that wrap partially around the building, so that it's possible to look up and down the street, and used generous openings around the stairs and double-height spaces when possible." All of these design tricks give the home an open and sprawling feel.

Because the firm provides both interior design and product design services, it was able to offer a cohesive finished product, with an emphasis on industrial chic. Floor materials range from terrazzo to ground concrete, gray limestone, and American walnut. In a creative use of factory-friendly textures, the entrance steps are covered with a leather runner typically used as a drive belt in mills. The gleaming kitchen features cabinets by Boffi and leather bar stools by Jim Zivic, and a counter in the same polished concrete found on the floors and stairs.

When the weather is nice, 12-by-12-foot kitchen doors pull back accordion-style, allowing the dining area to flow onto the deck for the perfect indoor-outdoor entertaining space. Guests can sit around the walnut table on chairs just inside or choose to chill out around the rain-resistant teak dining set designed by Baird, waiting for their hot dogs to come off the big built-in outdoor grill. (This European couple wanted to go American all the way and enjoy summer barbecues.) On the rooftop, Baird and his clients created the ultimate downtown urban leisure zone, with flooring in ipe, a fireplace, and a hot tub—an outdoor space that the family likes to use even during the winter.

**ABOVE** An extradeep granite Pietra Cardosa tub was the perfect fit for the children's bathroom. A jolt of bright blue Italian glass tile from Ann Sacks forms the backsplash.

**OPPOSITE** Pieces of blue limestone tile were stacked to create the beautiful fireplace à la Frank Lloyd Wright in the formal living room.

Delightfully contradictory, the home that presents a shielded face to the world is brilliantly suffused with light inside. A master bathroom on the top floor has both a cathedral skylight and a thick slab of cast glass beneath the sink, which filters daylight into the playroom below. Just above the massive 25-by-25-foot media room, more skylights illuminate a back wall. Here, built-in shelves hold books, photographs, and ceramics; the owners say that they like to keep all the potentially breakable items along one wall. Interchangeable stain-resistant duck sofa pieces from Troy fit together like Legos in the center of the room, on a concrete floor covered with a vegetable-dyed rug. One of the massive plaster walls is often used for projecting movies—in wide-screen, of course.

**ABOVE LEFT** Using teak, ipe, and zinc-coated copper, Baird created a city oasis for the family with easy access directly off the kitchen.

**ABOVE RIGHT** Space underneath the sidewalk above was carved out for a cave-like wine cellar. Baird popped upside-down wine bottles into the concrete for ingenious transference of light.

**OPPOSITE** Custom-made floor-to-ceiling bookcases cover one massive wall in the media room. A giant skylight floods the below-grade space with light from the terrace. An oil on canvas by Frank Brunner adorns the back wall above a graphic rug designed by Baird.

# RICHES SHARED

An invitation to a Denise Rich party billed as a "small and private" gathering may indeed be just that, or something a tad larger. In one instance, the guest list of a cozy get-together suddenly blossomed from a few dozen to 250. No problem for the hostess—the more, the merrier. Living in a huge duplex penthouse overlooking Fifth Avenue and Central Park means plenty of room for all. If need be, the private rooftop can be heated or tented, and the terrace transformed into an ice-skating rink, as was the case for a Grammy Awards party she hosted in the late 1990s.

A songwriter whose material had been recorded by artists including Céline Dion, Mary J. Blige, and Aretha Franklin, and who counts a galaxy of other musicians among her friends, Rich is a hostess deluxe whose high-profile gatherings bring in big names from the worlds of art, fashion, beauty, and politics. She's had fund-raisers for pals like Bill Clinton, but her number one cause is the G&P Charitable Foundation for Cancer Research . . . which has attracted the likes of Michael Jackson, Goldie Hawn, George Benson, and Wyclef Jean. (Her soirees always draw a diverse crowd—from Mikhail Gorbachev and Caroline Kennedy to Stevie Wonder and Placido Domingo.) Denise Rich has created a home environment spacious and glittering enough to accommodate the most fabulous event, and to make the most prestigious guests feel comfortable.

**OPPOSITE** Few collectors can display their own portrait by Julian Schnabel (*Portrait of Denise*, an oil, plates, and bondo on wood). Another Schnabel can be seen at left. Dappled light filters through a skylight over the antique mahogany dining table and the mahogany chairs from Philippe Farley.

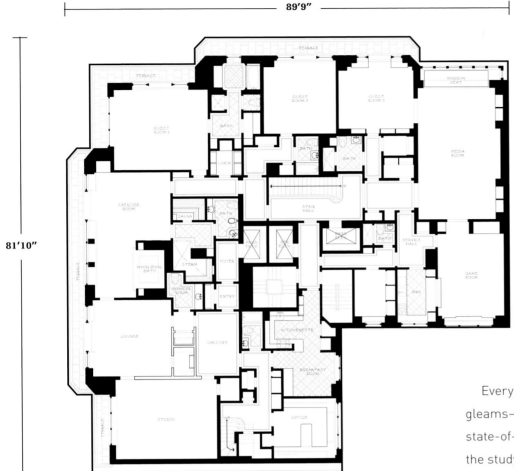

**ABOVE LEFT** Murray's detailed architectural drawing for the apartment's lower floor illustrates the vast maze of rooms.

**ABOVE RIGHT** "Our clients have a desire for larger informal areas now—like larger kitchens and wine storage," says Murray. Rich's French country kitchen can accommodate catering for six hundred or an intimate dinner for two.

**OPPOSITE** In the hallway to the private rooms, Murray popped in a trio of skylights illuminating pieces by Julian Schnabel to the right and Denise's daughter Ilona Malka Rich to the left.

Everything in this sweeping, 13,000-square-foot space gleams—from the superbuffed striated marble floors to the state-of-the-art kitchen to the mahogany-paneled walls of the study, where a Chagall hangs prominently above a marble fireplace, its joyous florals complementing a layering of photos of family and friends along the mantel and the bookshelves. Recessed lighting emphasizes marble and gold candelabras, gilded side tables, and huge framed artworks filling white-washed walls. Purchased in the mid-'90s, the home was originally a well-appointed one-bedroom box owned by a reclusive oil baron named Daniel Ludwig. Rich bought his apartment and the one just below at the same time, broke through the ceiling, and installed a staircase, which is now perfect for making grand entrances.

Right away, Rich made clear the purpose of the new home—namely, entertaining. What distinguishes this apartment from many other Manhattan showplaces is the variety to be found in the rooms: in the penthouse, 11-foot-high ceilings dominate, while rooms on the lower floors are just slightly less cavernous. The design challenge, then, was integrating the varied rooms

Photos of family and famous FODs (friends of Denise) decorate the sumptuous library. The rich walls are French-polished fiddleback mahogany with an ornamental plaster decorative diamond frieze. The overstuffed floral sofa is a nod to Marc Chagall's *Grand Bouquet* over the fireplace. To the right, behind the lamp, is a portrait by Peter Max of Denise's daughter Gabrielle.

so that a flow was achieved, and integrating the different functions of Rich's public life—from the entertaining spaces to the recording studio to her office for charity work—with the rooms designated for day-to-day life.

Soon after buying the two apartments, Rich purchased yet another (also on the top floor) and turned half of this level into her master suite and the rest into opulent yet comfortable public rooms, most of which share a drop-dead view of Central Park. A terrace snakes around the dining room on Fifth Avenue, along the long living room, then turns east to run back toward the cozy library, offering guests a rare outdoor perch fifty stories above Wollman Rink and the zoo.

From the beginning, the operative word was *expansiveness*. So many large glass windows needed to be installed that the contractor had to close down Fifth Avenue and place a crane in the middle of the street to hoist each of the huge pieces up to the penthouse level. Hardly intimidated by the size or scope, Rich wanted these rooms to be as large as possible to offer generous accommodation for guests. The approach, architecturally, was

**LEFT** A vast terrace winds its way around the upper level of the home, providing limitless views of Central Park. Andy Warhol's *4 Marilyns* can be seen at left; at right is a Paul Klee mobile.

**ABOVE** A side view of Rich's two floors and outrageous private rooftop garden, filled with landscaping, trees and potted plants, antique marble tables, and latticework.

to feature detailing that was traditional but pared down because the building is postwar. On the penthouse floor, door trims and casings needed to be scaled up to make them appropriate for big glass openings. These were not all egg-and-dart moldings— more important was the scale and the intricacy.

A starting point in the decorating process and an obvious thread of interior design continuity is Rich's eighteenth- and nineteenth-century furniture. A born shopper, Rich had no problem filling the home with a wide range of objects found during her travels around the world. "She likes antiques, modern things, contemporary art, beautiful rugs," says an interior designer friend. "She likes shiny, glamorous fabrics.

**ABOVE** A stately ebony Yamaha grand piano anchors the living room. The backdrop of Central Park provides the perfect setting for impromptu performances. A Persian rug, rarely seen in such a great size, provides an understated complement to the bold artworks by Miró, Léger, and Picasso.

**RIGHT** The opulent dining room features a mahogany table dating back to the late 1700s, over which hangs a Maria Theresa cut-crystal chandelier. Works by George Condo (left) and Pablo Picasso (far wall) vie for attention with the dazzling view.

If I called Denise a magpie, I mean it only in the best possible way. Hers is a luxurious magpie aesthetic. She's all about a bell and a whistle." The other visual that clearly connects the space is the world-class art collection, including pieces by Warhol, Schnabel, Picasso, Miró, and Chagall.

Under the direction of architect John B. Murray, the duplex was created with four bedrooms and an astounding eleven bathrooms. "I wanted to have a large family apartment and a personal writing and recording studio," says Rich, who has two grown children (a third child, Gabrielle, died of cancer in 1996 at the age of twenty-seven, motivating Rich to create the research foundation). "Having the studio in the apartment makes it easy to create when I have an idea." Patti LaBelle, Jessica Simpson, and Natalie Cole, among others, have recorded hits in this creative sanctuary. The dining room has seen past presidents and dignitaries seated around the Empire mahogany table. Under the Clinton administration, the president and the vice president attended a dinner here together (which, for reasons of national security, is a rarity!).

Ornate, regal, and feminine, this home wraps its residents and guests in luxury. And that's the joy of Denise Rich's apart-ment—her famous parties allow many to partake in her good fortune and glamorous style. She's big on sharing her riches.

**ABOVE LEFT AND RIGHT** Hit records by Natalie Cole and Céline Dion line the casual recording studio where Denise has written and recorded dozens of award-winning songs. Built-ins of French-polished cherrywood conceal the recording booth, adjacent to the high-tech mixing equipment.

**OPPOSITE** The richly appointed powder room is a study in reflective surfaces: Verdi green marble floors, a brass sink, and a Venetian mirror painted in gold, bronze, and silver, all emit a glow. A pair of rock crystal and gilt metal light sconces flank the mirror.

# RESOURCES

For information on specific pieces shown in this book, please see the page-by-page credits on page 252.

**A.M. COLLECTIONS**
584 Broadway, Suite 201
New York, NY 10012
212.625.2616
www.amcollections.com

**ABC CARPET & HOME**
888 Broadway
New York, NY 10003
212.473.3000
www.abchome.com

**ADAM FUSS**
Cheim & Read
547 West 25th Street
New York, NY 10001
212.242.7727
gallery@cheimread.com
www.cheimread.com

**AERO**
419 Broome Street
New York, NY 10012
212.966.4700

**ALAN MOSS**
436 Lafayette Street
New York, NY 10013
212.473.1310
www.alanmossny.com

**ALEX DALY ART**
American Custom Quilting
20 East 30th Street, Suite 2E
New York, NY 10016
212.679.0168
www.alexdaly.com

**ANDREAS GURSKY**
Metropolitan Museum of Art
1000 Fifth Avenue
New York, NY 10028
212.535.7710
www.metmuseum.org

**ANDRIANNA HOME**
121 Greene Street
New York, NY 10012
310.456.2243

**ANDY WARHOL**
Andy Warhol Foundation
65 Bleecker Street, #7
New York, NY 10012
212.387.7555
www.warholfoundation.org

**ANN SACKS**
204 East 58th Street
New York, NY 10022
800.278.8453
www.annsacks.com

**ANTIQUERIA TRIBECA**
129 Duane Street
New York, NY 10013
212.227.7500

**ARCHITECTURAL ARTIFACTS**
4325 North Ravenswood
Chicago, IL 60613
773.348.0622
www.architecturartifacts.com

**ARMANI CASA**
97 Greene Street
New York, NY 10012
212.334.1271
www.armanicasa.com

**ARTEMIDE**
1980 New Highway
Farmingdale, NY 11735
631.694.9292
www.artemide.us

**ASIA RUSTIC**
75 Franklin Street
New York, NY 10013
www.asiarustic.com

**AUBUSSON CARPET**
New York Design Center
200 Lexington Avenue
Suite 1006
New York, NY 10016
212.696.0080
info@renaissancecarpet.com
www.renaissancecarpet.com

**AUGUSTE RODIN**
Musée Rodin - 79, rue de Varenne
Paris, France 75007
33.0.1.44.18.61.10
www.musee-rodin.fr

**AUGUSTIN CARDENAS**
www.artnet.com

**B&B ITALIA**
150 East 58th Street
New York, NY 10155
800.872.1697
www.bebitalia.com

**BARON UPHOLSTERERS**
545 West 45th Street
New York, NY 10016
212.664.0800
info@baronnyc.com
www.baronnyc.com

**BED BATH & BEYOND**
620 Avenue of the Americas
New York, NY 10011
212.255.3550
www.bedbathandbeyond.com

**BERTOIA**
Bertoia @ Knoll Furniture
76 Ninth Avenue
New York, NY 10011
212.343.4000
jrivera@knoll.com
www.bertoiaharry.com

**BIEDERMEIER**
Swan House, Windmill Road
Sunbury on Thames, Middlesex, UK
TW16 7DT
01932.710.890
office@biedermeier.co.uk
www.biedermeier.co.uk

**BIELECKY BROTHERS**
R. Gasparre Custom Furniture, Inc.
32-45 62nd Street
Woodside, NY 11377
718.726.7348
www.gasparrecustomfurniture.com

**BLATT BILLIARDS**
809 Broadway
New York, NY 10003
212.674.8855
www.blattbilliards.com

**BMW**
www.bmw.com

**BOFFI**
85 Grand Street
New York, NY 10013
212.431.8282
www.boffi-soho.com

**BRUNSCHWIG & FILS**
75 Virginia Road
North White Plains, NY 10603
914.684.5800
staff@brunschwig.com
www.brunschwig.com

**BULTHAUP**
103 Eisenhower Pkwy, Suite 108
Roseland, NJ 07068
973.226.5390
www.bulthaup.com

**BURNING RELIC**
Jefferson, NY
607.652.9432
jimzivic@burningrelic.com
www.jimzivic.com

**C.I.T.E.**
131 Greene Street
New York, NY 10012
212.431.7272
www.citenyc.com

**CAESARSTONE**
6840 Hayvenhurst Avenue
Suite 100
Van Nuys, CA 91406
818.779.0999
info@caesarstoneus.com
www.caesarstoneus.com

**CANDIDA HOFER**
Rena Bransten Gallery
77 Geary Street
San Francisco, CA 94108
415.982.3292
info@renabranstengallery.com
www.renabranstengallery.com

**CAPPELLINI**
152 Wooster Street
New York, NY 10012
212.966.0669
www.cappellini.it

**CARINI LANG**
335 Greenwich Street
New York, NY 10013
646.613.0497
www.carinilang.com

**CARLO SCARPA**
www.artnet.com

**CAROLYN QUARTERMAINE FABRIC**
info@carolynquartermaine.com
www.carolynquartermaine.com

**CAROTTO**
154 NW 37th Street
Miami, FL 33127
305.573.2021

**CHARLES JACOBSEN**
c/o Pacific Design Center
8687 Melrose Avenue, G679
West Hollywood, CA 90069
310.652.1188
www.charlesjacobsen.com

**CHARLES SAUNDERS ANTIQUES**
255 Fulham Road
London, UK  SW3 6HY
020.7351.5242
www.charlessaundersantiques.co.uk

**CHISTA**
537 Greenwich Street
New York, NY 10013
212.924.0394
info@chista.net
www.chista.net

**CHRISTIAN LIAIGRE**
www.christian-liaigre.fr

**CHRISTIE'S**
20 Rockefeller Center
New York, NY 10020
212.636.2000
www.christies.com

**COSTELLO STUDIO**
21-07 41st Avenue, 4th Floor
Long Island City, NY 11101
718.383.8108
www.csidesigns.com

**CRATE AND BARREL**
611 Broadway
New York, NY 10012
212.780.0004
www.crateandbarrel.com

**DAMIEN HIRST**
Gagosian Gallery
555 West 24th Street
New York, NY 10011
212.741.1111
newyork@gagosian.com
www.gagosian.com

**DAN DAVIDSON ART**
www.artnet.com

**DAN FLAVIN**
The Dan Flavin Art Institute
Corwith Avenue
Bridgehampton, NY
212.989.5566, ext. 518

**DANIEL ROMUALDEZ ARCHITECTS**
119 West 23rd Street
New York, NY 10011
212.989.8429

**DAVID EASTON**
5 Union Square West
New York, NY 10003
212.334.3820
www.davideastoninc.com

**DAVID SMYTH**
www.artnet.com

**DAVID WEEKS**
68 Jay Street, #612A
Brooklyn, NY 11201
718.596.7945
info@davidweeksstudio.com
www.davidweeksstudio.com

**DECO BY REGINA**
Regina Nuessle
1629 Jefferson Avenue
Miami Beach, FL 33139
305.375.0727
regina@decobyregina.com
www.decobyregina.com

**DIRECTIONS**
3801 West Reno Avenue
Oklahoma City, OK 73107
405.948.7978

**DONALD JUDD FURNITURE**
Louisa Guinness Gallery
99 Oxford Gardens
London, UK W10 6NF
020.7734.8888
www.louisaguinnessgallery.com

**DORNBRACHT FAUCETS**
PO Box 1454
D-58584
Iserlohn, Germany
49.0.23.71.433.0
mail@dornbracht.de
www.dornbracht.com

**DOROTHY DRAPER**
60 East 56th Street
New York, NY 10022
212.758.2810
dorothydraperco@dorothydraper.com
www.dorothydraper.com

**DOYLE ANTIQUES**
711 Warren Street
Hudson, NY 12534
518.828.3929
www.hudsoncityantiques.net

**DUTRUC-ROSSET**
12, rue Beranger
75003 Paris, France
33.142.72.13.31

**EAMES @ MOSS**
50 Greene Street
New York, NY 10012
212.204.7100

**EBANISTA**
Merchandise Mart
222 Merchandise Mart Plaza
Suite 1677
Chicago, IL 60654
312.822.0323
chicago@ebanista.com
www.ebanista.com

**ECLECTIC ELEMENTS**
2227 Coral Way
Miami, FL 33145
305.285.0899
www.eemiami.net

**ED WORMLEY FOR DUNBAR**
P.O. Box 5541
High Point, NC 27262
336.734.1700
service@collectdunbar.com
www.collectdunbar.com

**EDELMAN**
Edelman Leather
979 Third Avenue
2nd Floor
New York, NY 10022
212.751.3339
cherylm@edelmanleather.com
www.edelmanleather.com

**EILEEN GRAY**
MoMA
11 West 53rd Street
New York, NY 10019
212.708.9400
www.moma.org

**ELIZABETH STREET ANTIQUES**
210 Elizabeth Street
New York, NY 10012
212.644.6969

**EMMERSON TROOP**
8111 Beverly Boulevard
Los Angeles, CA 90048
323.653.9763
info@emmersontroop.com
www.emmersontroop.com

**FISCHER FURNITURE**
361 Stagg Street, Suite #3L
Brooklyn, NY 11206
718.418.6206
fischerfurniture@nyc.rr.com

**FLEXFORM**
via Einaudi 23/25
20036 Meda, Italy
+0362.3991
info@flexform.it
www.flexform.it

**FORTUNY**
979 Third Avenue, Suite 1632
New York, NY 10022
212.753.7153
www.fortuny.com

**FRANK BRUNNER**
www.frankbrunner.net

**FRETTE**
41 East Oak Street
Chicago, IL 60611
312.649.3744
frette_chicago@frette.com
www.frette.com

**FRITZ HANSEN**
Allerødvej 8
3450 Allerød, Denmark
45.4817.2300
www.fritzhansen.com

**FUTURAMA**
446 North LaBrea Avenue
Los Angeles, CA 90036
323.937.4522
www.futuramafurniture.net

**GRACIE, J.M. SHEA**
419 Lafayette Street
New York, NY 10003
212.924.6816
www.graciestudio.com

**GREENE STREET ANTIQUES**
76 Wooster Street
New York, NY 10012
212.274.1076

**GUGGENHEIM MUSEUM**
1071 Fifth Avenue
New York, NY 10128
212.423.3500
visitorinfo@guggenheim.org
www.guggenheim.org

**GUINEVERE ANTIQUES**
574-580 Kings Road
London, UK SW6 2DY
020.7736.2917
Sales@guinevere.co.uk
www.guinevere.co.uk

**HANSGROHE FIXTURES**
1490 Bluegrass Lakes Parkway
Alpharetta, GA 30004
800.488.8119
www.hansgrohe-usa.com

**HERB RITTS FOUNDATION**
P.O. Box 1618
Los Angeles, CA 90078
thefoundation@herbritts.com
www.herbritts.com

**HOLLY HUNT**
979 Third Avenue
Suite 503/605
New York, NY 10022
212.755.6555
www.hollyhunt.com

**HOPE'S WINDOWS**
84 Hopkins Avenue
P.O. Box 580
Jamestown, NY 14702
716.665.5124
www.hopeswindows.com

**HORST PHOTOGRAPHY**
1629 NE 1st Avenue
Miami, FL 33132
info@GalerieVolkerDiehl.com
www.horstphorst.com

**IKEA**
800.434.4532
www.ikea.com

**INGO MAUER**
89 Grand Street
New York, NY 10013
212.965.8817
making-light@ingomaurer-usa.com
www.ingomauer.com

**INTERIOR DYNAMICS**
1742 Crooks Road
Troy, MI 48084
800.935.3962
www.interiordynamics.com

**IRREPLACABLE ARTIFACTS**
428 Main Street
Middletown, CT 06457
860.344.8576
www.demolitiondepot.com

**JACK PIERSON PHOTOGRAPHY**
Cheim & Read
547 West 25th Street
New York, NY 10001
212.242.7727

**JACQUES CARCANAGUES**
21 Greene Street
New York, NY 10012
212.925.8110
carcan@jcarcan.com
jacquescarcanaguesinc.1stdibs.com

**JEAN-MICHEL BASQUIAT**
Gagosian Gallery
980 Madison Avenue
New York, NY 10021
212.744.2313
www.gagosian.com

**JEFF KOONS**
601 West 29th Street
New York, NY 10001
212.226.2894
www.jeffkoonsart.com

**JEFF WALL**
Marian Goodman Gallery
24 West 57th Street
New York, NY 10019
212.977.7160
goodman@mariangoodman.com
www.mariangoodman.com/mg/nyc.htm

**JIM MISNER LIGHT DESIGNS**
Montage
78 Arlington Street
Boston, MA 02116
415-928-0400
info@jimmisnerlightdesigns.com
www.montageweb.com

**JOHN FISCHER**
361 Stagg Street, Suite #3L
Brooklyn, NY 11206
718.418.6206
fischerfurniture@nyc.rr.com

**JONNY DETIGER**
369 Broadway, #412
New York, NY 10013
212.723.2811
jonny@jonnydetiger.com
www.jonnydetiger.com

**KARGES**
1501 W. Maryland Street
Evansville, IN 47710
812.425.2291
www.karges.com

**KEITH HARING**
676 Broadway
New York, NY 10012
www.haring.com

**KERRY JOYCE**
115 North LaBrea Avenue
Los Angeles, CA 90036
323.938.4442
info@kerryjoyce.com
www.kerryjoyce.com

**KEVIN REILLY**
c/o Isabelle Goughenheim
Chicago, IL
773.235.8909
isabelle@kevinreillylighting.com
www.kevinreillylighting.com

**KID ROBOT**
118 Prince Street
New York, NY 10012
212.966.6688
nystore@kidrobot.com
www.kidrobot.com

**KNOLL**
76 Ninth Avenue, Floor 11
New York, NY 10011
212.343.4000
nyc@knoll.com
www.knoll.com

**KOHLER**
800.456.4537
www.kohler.com

**KONAN**
665 88th Street
Brooklyn, NY 11220
718.680.7277

**KRAVET**
222 Central Avenue South
Bethpage, NY 11714
516.293.2000
customer.service@kravet.com
www.e-designtrade.com

**LA MURRINA**
Murano Designer Lighting, Inc.
8925 Beverly Boulevard
Los Angeles, CA 90048
310.858.7080
www.lamurrina.us

**LE CORNUE RANGE**
Krup's Kitchen & Bath
11 West 18th Street
New York, NY 10011
212.243.5787
www.lacornue.com

**LEE JOFA**
6-136 Merchandise Mart
Chicago, IL 60654
312.644.2965
www.leejofa.com

**LIGHT LAB**
1 Technology Park Drive
Westford, MA 01886
978.399.1000
sales@lightlabimaging.com
www.lightlabimaging.com

**LIGNE ROSET**
155 Wooster Street
New York, NY 10012
212.253.5629
www.lignerosetny.com

**MARC CHAGALL**
MoMA
11 West 53rd Street
New York, NY 10019
212.708.9400
www.moma.org

**MARTYN LAWRENCE BULLARD**
8101 Melrose Avenue
Los Angeles, CA 90046
323.655.5080
info@martynlawrencebullard.com
www.martynlawrencebullard.com

**MARVIN ALEXANDER**
315 East 62nd Street
New York, NY 10065
212.838.2320
ma@marvinalexanderinc.com
www.marvinalexanderinc.com

**MATT BAIRD ARCHITECTS**
250 Hudson Street
13th Floor
New York, NY 10013
212.334.2499
www.bairdarchitects.com

**MCKINLEY PIERRE FURNITURE**
5050 74th Avenue, Unit C
Miami, FL 33166
786.728.0906
www.mckinleypierre.com

**MICHELE VARIAN**
35 Crosby Street
New York, NY 10013
212.343.0033
www.michelevarian.com

**MIES VAN DER ROHE BARCELONA CHAIRS**
336 Bon Air Center #112
Greenbrae, CA 94904
888.743.8832
info@thefurniturecollection.com
www.barcelonachair.com

**MISON CONCEPTS**
485-33 South Broadway
Hicksville, NY 11801
516.933.8000
www.mison.com

**MODERNICA**
7366 Beverly Blvd.
Los Angeles, CA 90036
323.933.0380
lashowroom@modernica.net
www.modernica.net

**MODERNISM GALLERY**
800 Douglas Road, Suite 101
Coral Gables, FL 33134
888.217.2760
artdeco@modernism.com
www.modernism.com

**MOLLER WILLRICH DESIGN**
San Francisco, CA
415.885.4330
mw@moller-willrich.com
www.moller-willrich.com

**MOSS**
150 Greene Street
New York, NY 10012
866.888.6677
store@mossonline.com
www.mossonline.com

**NANCY CORZINE FURNITURE**
979 Third Avenue
New York, NY 10022
212.223.8340
nancycor.ipower.com

**NEW YORK BOTANICAL GARDEN**
200th Street and Kazimiroff Blvd.
Bronx, NY 10458
718.817.8700
www.nybg.org

**OLD WORLD WEAVERS**
979 Third Avenue
New York, NY 10022
212.752.9000
www.starkfabric.com/OWW

**OSBORNE & LITTLE FABRIC**
90 Commerce Road
Stamford, CT 06902
203.359.1500
www.osborneandlittle.com

**PARIS FLEA MARKET**
140, rue des Rosiers
93400 Saint-Ouen, France
01.40.12.32.58
www.parispuces.com

**PAUL FERRANTE**
8464 Melrose Place
Los Angeles, CA 90069
323.653.4142
info@paulferrante.com
www.paulferrante.com

**PAUL KLEE**
Guggenheim Museum Store
1071 Fifth Avenue
New York, NY 10128
212.423.3500
www.guggenheim.org

**PAUL SMITH ART**
142 Greene Street
New York, NY 10012
mail@paulsmithart.com
www.paulsmithart.com

**PETER MAX ART**
customersupport@petermax.com
www.petermax.com

**PHILLIP JEFFRIES LTD.**
Tennant & Associates
Michigan Design Center
1700 Stutz Drive, Suite 61
Troy, MI 48084
248.643.6140
www.michigandesign.com
www.phillipjeffries.com

**PHILIPPE STARCK**
Paasheuvelweg 16
1105 BH Amsterdam ZO
Netherlands
33.0.1.48.07.54.54
projects@starcknetwork.com
www.philippe-starck.com

**PHOENIX DAY**
c/o Tui Pranich & Assoc.
979 Third Avenue, #1520
New York, NY 10022
212.980.6173
newyork@tuipranichassociates.com

**PIET BOON ZONE**
Ambacht 6
1511 JZ Oostzaan
Amsterdam, Netherlands
31.075.655.9000
info@pietboon.nl
www.pietboon.nl

**POLIFORM**
150 East 58th Street
6th Floor
New York, NY 10155
888.POLIFORM
www.poliformusa.com

**PORSCHE**
c/o Manhattan Motorcars
262-270 Eleventh Avenue
New York, NY 10001
888.810.7419
www.manhattan.porschedealer.com

**POTTERY BARN**
100-104 Seventh Avenue
New York, NY 10011
646.336.7160
www.potterybarn.com

**PUTNAM LADDER COMPANY**
32 Howard Street
New York, NY 10013
212-226-5147
www.putnamrollingladder.com

**RALPH LAUREN HOME**
379 West Broadway
New York, NY 10012
212.625.1660
www.ralphlaurenhome.com

**RALPH PUCCI**
44 West 18th Street
New York, NY 10011
212.633.0452
www.ralphpucci.net

**REMAINS ANTIQUE LIGHTING**
130 West 28th Street
New York, NY 10001
212.675.8051
www.remains.com

**REWIRE**
442 North LaBrea Avenue
Los Angeles, CA 90036
323.937.5254
www.rewirela.com

**RICHARD SERRA**
MoMA
11 West 53rd Street
New York, NY 10019
212.708.9400
www.moma.org

**RITTER ANTIK**
35 East 10th Street
New York, NY 10003
212.673.2213
www.ritterantik.com

**ROBERT ABBEY**
3166 Main Avenue S.E.
Hickory, NC 28602
828.322.3480
www.robertabbey.com

ROGERS & GOFFIGON
545 West 45th Street
New York, NY 10016
212.664.0800

ROMAN THOMAS
www.romanthomas.com

ROOM SERVICE
5901 West 3rd Street
Los Angeles, CA 90036
323.692.9221
sales@roomservicestore.com
www.roomservicestore.com

ROSE BOWL FLEA MARKET
1001 Rose Bowl Drive
Pasadena, CA 91103
www.rgcshows.com

ROY KINZER PAINTING
Denise Bibro Fine Arts
529 West 20th Street
4th Floor
New York, NY 10011
212.647.7030
www.roykinzer.com

RUDI PILLEN
www.rudipillen.be

S & S FABRIC
1 Maritime Drive
Portsmouth, RI 02871
800.441.2252
info@ssfabricproducts.com
www.ssfabricproducts.com

SAM ROBIN
100 Venetian Way
Suite 112
Miami, FL 33139
305.375.0727
srinterior@samrobin.com
www.samrobin.com

SANTA MONICA FLEA MARKET
Santa Monica Airport
Airport Avenue off Bundy
Los Angeles, CA 90405
323.933.2511

SANTE D'ORAZIO
611 Broadway, Suite 625
New York, NY 10012
212.420.0488
diane@santedorazio.com
www.santedorazio.com

SARAJO
130 Greene Street
New York, NY 10012
212.966.6156

SAXONY CARPET
D&D Building
979 Third Avenue
Suite 1400
New York, NY 10022
212.239.7990
info@saxcarpet.com
www.saxcarpet.com

SCALAMANDRÉ
300 Trade Zone Drive
Ronkonkoma, NY 11779
631.467.8800
info@scalamandre.com
www.scalamandre.com

SCHNELLER & SONS
129 West 29th Street
New York, NY 10001
212.695.9440

SERIOUS CLOTHING
7569 Melrose Avenue
Los Angeles, CA 90046
323.655.0589
www.seriousclothing.com

SHIN AZUMI
12A Vicars Road
London, UK NW5 4NL
44.0.20.7428.7501
info@shinazumi.com

SIRIO
by Sam Robin
100 Venetian Way
Suite 112
Miami, Fl 33139
305.375.0727
srinterior@samrobin.com
www.samrobin.com

SOTHEBY'S
1334 York Avenue
New York, NY 10021
212.606.7000
www.sothebys.com

SPENCER FINCH
Rona Hoffman Gallery
118 North Peoria Street
Chicago, IL 60607
312.455.1990
rhoffman@rhoffmangallery.com
www.rhoffmangallery.com

SPINNEYBECK
425 Crosspoint Parkway, #100
Getzville, NY 14068
800.482.5555
sales@spinneybeck.com
www.spinneybeck.com

STARK
979 Third Avenue
New York, NY 10022
212.752.9000
info@starkcarpet.com
www.starkcarpet.com
www.starkfabric.com

STARN TWINS
64 Union Street
Brooklyn, NY 11231
718.522.7027
www.starnstudio.com

STEINWAY & SONS
109 West 57th Street
New York, NY 10019
212.246.1100
showrooms@steinway.com
www.steinway.com

STONEGATE
4200 Niles Road
St. Joseph, MI 49085
269.429.8328
www.stonegatedesigns.com

STRATUM TEXTILES
3836 Willat Avenue
Culver City, CA 90232
310.280.5610
www.stratumtextiles.com

SUB-ZERO
Westye Group
150 East 58th Street
5th Floor
New York, NY 10155
212.207.9223
www.subzerowolfeast.com

SWEET SMILING HOME
1317 Palmetto Street
Los Angeles, CA 90013
213.687.9630
www.sweetsmilinghome.com

TAMA
5 Harrison Street
New York, NY 10003
212.566.7030
www.tamagallery.com

TEL AVIV MUSEUM
27 Shaul Hamelech Boulevard
Tel Aviv, Israel 64329
www.tamuseum.com

TERRA VERDE FLOORING
3169 Shipps Corner Road
Suites 101-103
Virginia Beach, VA 23453
757.689.4614
www.terraverdeflooring.com

THASSOS MARBLE
Athenian Marble
369 Syngroy Avenue, P. Phaleron
175 64 Athens, Greece
30.1.94.800.48/9
sales@thassosmarble.com
www.thassosmarble.com

THE ABADJIAN COLLECTION
200 Lexington Avenue
Suite 1001
New York, NY 10016
212.683.2043

THE CARPET BOUTIQUE
96A NE 40th Street
Miami, FL 33137
305.325.1919

THERMADOR
5551 McFadden Avenue
Huntington Beach, CA 92649
800.656.9226
www.thermador.com

THOMAS STRUTH
Marian Goodman Gallery
24 West 57th Street
New York, NY 10019
212.977.7160
www.mariangoodman.com

TOM THOMAS GALLERY
318 East 59th Street
New York, NY 10022
212.688.6100
www.tomthomasgallery.com

TORD BOONTJE
Moss
150 Greene Street
New York, NY 10012
212.204.7100
www.mossonline.com

TRIARCH
42 North Moore
New York, NY 10013
212.431.1455
email@triarch.com
www.triarch.com

UGO RONDINONE
New Museum Store
235 Bowery
New York, NY 10002
212.219.1222
www.newmuseum.org

URBAN ARCHAEOLOGY
143 Franklin Street
New York, NY 10013
212.431.4646
www.urbanarchaeology.com

VIKING
111 Front Street
Greenwood, MI 38930
888.845.4641
www.vikingrange.com

VINCENT MULFORD
417 Warren Street
Hudson, NY 12534
518.828.5489
www.vmulford.com

VOLA
Lunavej 2
8700 Horsens, Denmark
45.7023.5500
sales@vola.dk
www.vola.dk

WATERWORKS
469 Broome Street
New York, NY 10013
212.966.0605
www.waterworks.com

WIFREDO LAM ART
Gallery Gertrude Stein
200 West 57th Street
New York, NY 10019
212.535.0600
www.gallerygertrudestein.com

WOKA VIENNA
Palais Breuner
Singerstrasse 16
A-1010 Vienna, Austria
43.1.513.29.12
info@woka.com
www.woka.com

WOLF
150 East 58th Street
5th Floor
New York, NY 10155
212.207.9223
www.subzerowolfeast.com

WYETH
315 Spring Street
New York, NY 10013
212.243.3661

WYSTERIA
41 Fifth Avenue, Suite 1E
New York, NY 10003
646.522.7810
www.wysterianyc.com

YAMAHA PIANOS
6600 Orangethorpe Avenue
Buena Park, CA 90620
800.854.1569
www.yamaha.com

# CREDITS For contact information for specific vendors, please see the Resources (page 248).

**PAGE 2:** Sofa and club chairs: B&B Italia; fixtures: Moss; artwork: David Smyth

**PAGE 5:** Wall hanging: Thomas Struth

**PAGE 6:** Barcelona chairs: Mies van der Rohe for Design Within Reach; white vinyl chair: Rose Bowl Flea Market

**PAGE 8:** Fixture: David Weeks; arm chairs: Ralph Pucci

**PAGE 11:** Area rug: Aubusson Carpet; window treatments: Marvin Alexander

**PAGE 15:** Staircase: Joe Jaroff

**PAGES 16-17:** Armoire: Daniel Romualdez Architects; vitrine: Joe Jaroff; carpet: Carini Lang; artwork: Andrew Polk (left)

**PAGE 18-19:** Cabinetry: Boffi; ladder: Putnam Ladder Company; range: Viking; refrigerator: Sub-Zero

**PAGE 20-21:** Sofa and chairs: ABC Carpet & Home; artwork (on brick wall): Doug & Mike Starn; red upholstered chairs: Crate & Barrel; rug: Pottery Barn; glass lamp: Sarajo

**PAGE 22, below:** Landscape architecture: Patricia Cobb; outdoor furnishings: Kingsley-Bate

**PAGE 24, left:** Counters and floor tiles: Urban Archaeology; fixtures: Waterworks; rug: El Paso Trading Company

**PAGES 24-27:** Piano: Steinway & Sons; lounger: Mies van der Rohe; sofa and Barcelona chairs: B&B Italia

**PAGE 32:** Wood Bench: Eclectic Elements

**PAGE 35:** Couches: McKinley Pierre Furniture

**PAGES 36-37:** Appliances: GE Monogram; countertops: LPC

**PAGE 39, right:** Daybed: Eclectic Elements; flooring: Interceramic Corp.; rug: Ido

**PAGE 41:** Sofa and club chairs: Donghia

**PAGES 42-43:** Sofa: Kevin Gray Designs

**PAGE 45:** French daybed: Kevin Gray Designs

**PAGES 46-47:** Tables: Crate & Barrel; upholstery: Bergamo

**PAGE 54, left:** Rug: Old World Weavers

**PAGES 54-55:** Upholstery: Scalamandré

**PAGE 58, below:** Carpet: Stark; upholstery: Old World Weavers

**PAGES 60-61:** Carpet: Stark; wallcoverings, window treatments and bed linens: Scalamandré

**PAGES 64-65:** Wallcoverings and window treatments: Old World Weavers; chair fabric: Scalamandré

**PAGE 69:** Shelving and doors: Nick Mongiardo of Decorative Arts

**PAGES 70-71:** Piano: Steinway

**PAGES 72-73:** Staircase: 1100 Architects; runner: Stark

**PAGE 74-75:** Sconces: Emily Todhunter; sofa: Coolhouse

**PAGES 76-77:** Rug: ABC Carpet & Home; daybed: André Arbus; Ruhlmann secrétaire: Holly Johnson

**PAGE 79:** Fixture: Rose Bowl Flea Market

**PAGES 80-81:** Barcelona Chairs: Mies van der Rohe for Design Within Reach

**PAGE 82:** Bench: Sweet Smiling Home; fixture: Harlem Architectural Salvage

**PAGE 83:** Pew: Santa Monica Flea Market

**PAGES 84-85:** Artwork: Zoe; bed: Ikea

**PAGE 86:** Pod chair: Modernica; stand: Futurama; fixture: Room Service

**PAGE 87:** Sofa and club chairs: B&B Italia; fixtures: Moss

**PAGES 88-89:** Carpets: Rose Bowl Flea Market

**PAGE 90:** Chairs: Christian Liaigre; flowerpot sculpture: Donald Baechler

**PAGE 91—113:** Bench: MaxPouf by Piet Boon; fixtures: Brand van Egmond

**PAGES 92-93:** Kitchen: Poliform

**PAGE 93, right:** Sink: Piet Boon

**PAGES 96-97:** Sofa and arm chairs: Flexform; coffee table: B&B Italia

**PAGE 98:** Sofas: B&B Italia

**PAGE 99:** White vase: Mobach; window treatment: Jan Schouten

**PAGE 100-101:** Headboard: Piet Boon; lamp: Tord Boontje

**PAGE 103:** Photography: Thomas Struth

**PAGE 104:** Lighting: Light Lab; bench: Keith Haring; chair: Richard Artschwager

**PAGE 105:** Wall coverings: Holly Hunt; artwork: Spencer Finch

**PAGES 106-107:** Pendant light: Louis Poulsen; bar stools: Ligne Roset; countertop: Thassos Marble; cabinetry: Boffi; range: Viking

**PAGE 108:** Sofa: Michael Richman; lounge chair: Hans Wagner; upholstery: Classic Cloth

**PAGE 109, below:** Chair: Dan Flavin

**PAGES 110-111:** Sofa: Brueton; fabric: Glant; Lucid coffee table: Michael Richman; chairs: André Sorney

**PAGES 112-113:** Bathtub system: Boffi; flooring and countertop: Thassos Marble

**PAGE 115:** Wall art: Jonny Detiger

**PAGES 116-117:** Drums: Tama; sofa and chairs: Ligne Roset

**PAGE 118:** Range and refrigerator: Thermador

**PAGE 119:** Sofa: Ligne Roset

**PAGE 120, left:** Faucets: Kohler; fixtures: Vola

**PAGES 120-121:** Wall Art: Jonny Detiger

**PAGE 122, right:** Fixtures: Vola; bathtub: Waterworks

**PAGES 124-125:** Wall art: Jonny Detiger (right); drums: Tama

**PAGES 130-131:** Table: Paris Flea Market

**PAGES 132-133:** Window treatments: Caroline Quartermaine Fabrics

**PAGE 134, left:** Chandeliers: Paris Flea Market; window treatments: Caroline Quartermaine Fabrics

**PAGES 134-135:** Pendant Light: Fortuny

**PAGES 136-137:** Palm-Leaf Side Table: Ralph Lauren

**PAGE 138:** Light fixtures: Jim Misner Light Designs; range: La Cornue; shelving; Moller Willrich Design

**PAGE 139:** Windows: Moller Willrich Design

**PAGE 141:** Sofas: Armani Casa; artwork: Jeff Koons

**PAGES 142-143:** "Forever" artwork: Webster & Noble; butterfly artwork: Damien Hirst; fixtures: Maurer; dining table and chairs: Cappellini; sofa: Armani Casa

**PAGE 144:** Outdoor window structure: Wayne Turett Architecture

**PAGE 145, above:** Sofa: Armani Casa

**PAGE 146:** Leather furnishings: Ligne Roset; piano: Steinway & Sons; artwork: Richard Serra (left) and Ugo Rondinone (far wall)

**PAGE 148:** Bedding and mink throw: Ralph Lauren

**PAGES 148-149:** Tulip table: Knoll; chairs and standing lamp: Moss; T-shirt rug: ABC Carpet & Home

**PAGE 153:** Sofa: Lee Joffa; table: Interior Dynamics

**PAGES 156-157:** Furnishings: David Easton; coffee table: Costello Studio

**PAGE 160:** Table: Sotheby's; carpeting: Scalamandré: lighting: Kravet; fixtures: Marvin Alexander

**PAGE 161:** Fridge: Sub-Zero; range and dual Stove: Viking

**PAGE 162:** Table: Saunders Antiques; armoire: Guinevere Antiques; rug: JM Shea Gracie

**PAGE 163, below:** Window treatments: Baron Upholsterers; pillows: Stratum Textiles; chair: A.M. Collections; bedding: Frette

**PAGE 169:** Chairs: Eames by Moss

**PAGES 170-171:** Artwork: Kim MacConnell

**PAGES 172-173:** Artwork: Kim MacConnell(left); Jean-Michel Basquiat (framed drawing, right)

**PAGE 174:** Lamp: Kim MacConnell

**PAGE 176:** Furnishings: Dorothy Draper Consoles

**PAGE 178:** Console table: Coconut & Company; chairs: Aero

**PAGE 179:** Headboard: Aero

**PAGES 180-181:** Island: Aero; range: Viking

**PAGE 182:** Upholstered sofa: Thomas O'Brien

**PAGE 183:** Benches: Aero; window treatments: Thomas O'Brien

**PAGES 186-187:** Windows: Hope's Windows

**PAGE 187, right:** Window treatments: Thomas O'Brien

**PAGE 189:** Fixture: David Weeks

**PAGE 190-191:** Coffee table: Cascata; rug: Stark

**PAGE 192:** Fixture: David Weeks; sofa fabric: S&S Fabrics; coffee table: Chista; rug: Stark carpet; lamp: Sirio

**PAGE 193, left:** Club chair: Spinneybeck; rug: The Carpet Boutique

**PAGES 194-195:** Dining Table: Sirio

**PAGES 196-197:** Chairs: Sam Robin, lamp: MoMA

**PAGE 201:** Appliances: Bulthaup; stools: Shin Azumi

**PAGE 202:** Pool table: Triarch by Blatt Billiards; fixtures: Dutruc-Rosset

**PAGES 204-205:** Armoire: Kerry Joyce

**PAGES 206-208:** Carpet: Sotheby's; sofa and chairs: Kerry Joyce

**PAGE 209:** Footboard: Jean Michel Frank at Christie's; chairs: Biedermeier

**PAGE 213:** Sofa: Holly Hunt

**PAGE 217:** Table: Armani Casa; basket fixtures: Rewire

**PAGE 222, below:** Headboard fabric: Edelman; mirrors: Charles Jacobsen

**PAGE 223:** Sconces: Charles Jacobsen; cabinet pulls and stool: Andrianna Home

**PAGE 224:** Sofa: Troy; upholstery: Donghia; carpet: Tai Ping

**PAGES 226-227:** Fridge: Sub-Zero; cabinetry: Boffi

**PAGE 229:** Matt Baird Architecture; runner: Burning Relic

**PAGES 230-231:** Fridge: Sub-Zero; cabinetry: Boffi

**PAGE233:** Tub: Pietra Cardosa; tile: Ann Sacks

**PAGE 235:** Artwork: Frank Brunner; rug: Baird Designs

**PAGE 237:** Chairs: Philippe Farley; artwork: Julian Schnabel

**Page 238:** Artwork: Ilona Malka Rich (left), Julian Schnabel (right)

**PAGES 240-241:** Artwork: Marc Chagall (left), Peter Max (behind lamp), Andy Warhol (right)

**PAGES 242-243:** Artwork: Andy Warhol (left), Paul Klee mobile (right)

**PAGE 244, left:** Piano: Yamaha, artwork: Joan Miró (left wall), Fernand Léger (facing wall at left), Pablo Picasso (facing wall at right)

**PAGES 244-245:** Artwork: Pablo Picasso (right), George Condo (left)

**PAGE 246:** Tile: Verdi Flooring

**252** | CREDITS